THE 1993 TAX ACT

How the New Legislation Can Pay Off for You

Peter M. Berkery

IRWIN
Professional Publishing
Burr Ridge, Illinois
New York, New York

This publication is designed to provide accurate and authoritative information in regard to the subject matter covered. It is sold with the understanding that neither the author nor the publisher is engaged in rendering legal, accounting, or other professional service. If legal advice or other expert assistance is required, the services of a competent professional person should be sought.

From a Declaration of Principles jointly adopted by a Committee of the American Bar Association and a Committee of Publishers.

Sponsoring editor:	Michael E. Desposito
Project editor:	Jane Lightell
Production manager·	Bob Lange
Designer:	Heidi J. Baughman
Typeface.	11/13 Times Roman
Printer:	Arcata Graphics, Kingsport

Printed in the United States of America

1 2 3 4 5 6 7 8 9 0 AGK 0 9 8 7 6 5 4 3

ACKNOWLEDGEMENTS

I am indebted to several people for making this book a reality. First, I extend my gratitude to my editor, Mike Desposito, and his co-workers at Irwin for their guidance and encouragement. Expert technical review was provided by the "eagle eyes" of Jeff Lear and Gary Greene at the National Society of Public Accountants, by Professor Chuck Konkol of University of Wisconsin - Milwaukee, and by Keith Fevurly of the College for Financial Planning in Denver. Lillian Lea of Berkeley, California, shared her expertise in the tax -- and human -- consequences of natural disasters. Also thanks to mom and dad, Jean and Peter Berkery, who made sure my writing could be understood by "real people". Carl Cipra provided much-needed instruction in the intricacies of desktop publishing software. Most importantly, I am eternally grateful to my partner, Greg Diggins, who, as always, kept me and this project together.

INTRODUCTION

The Omnibus Budget Reconciliation Act of 1993 -- referred to throughout this book as "OBRA 93" -- is probably the most talked-about tax bill in several years. In partisan terms, it represents the largest aggregate increase in income taxes in the nation's history. This is undeniably true, but it only tells part of the story; *whose* taxes were raised is just as important to most taxpayers as *that* taxes were raised.

To the credit of its proponents, OBRA also represents the most serious effort to date to rein in the Federal government's astronomical budget deficit. Whether the steps toward that end were correct -- or sufficient -- remains to be seen, but the current cast of characters were, in fact, more honest and in earnest in addressing this pivotal issue than any of their predecessors.

OBRA did, in fact, make a host of changes to the tax law. The most publicized of these changes involve tax increases, some of them hefty. It also made a number of very specific pro-taxpayer changes; you have to be able to jump through the right hoops to be able to take advantage of them though. This book is intended to help you understand where OBRA hurts you, and where you can make the new legislation pay off for you.

*****

I've tried to write this book in simple, easy-to-understand english. That's not always easy when you're talking taxes, so a brief discussion of terminology is in order.

Generally. In order to make the basrc concepts ın this book understandable to real people, I've has to eliminate references to a lot of the technicalities of the particular portion of the law being discussed. While this should pose no bar to your understanding the basic parameters of a particular point of law, remember there are almost always exceptions. When you see the word generally, take it to heart

Income and *Taxable Income.* Income and taxable income are not the same thing. When the word income appears in the text, it generally refers to your income before deduction. By contrast, taxable income is the portion of your income you actually pay taxes on; its net of your deductions. It's important to understand and recognize the difference when your reading this book. Remember, you don't pay tax on your income, you pay tax on your taxable income. Get it?

Standard Deduction versus *Itemized Deduction.* Individual taxpayers are allowed to deduct certain expenses from their income in computing their taxable income. Most of us know these deductions as things like medical expenses (above a certain limit), state and local income taxes, real estate taxes, mortgage interest, charitable contributions, un-reimbursed business expenses incurred on behalf of our employers (above certain limits), expenses for business-related moves, investment expenses, casualty losses (above certain limits) and gambling losses (within limits). There are two ways of claiming these expenses. You can either list them all for the IRS on Schedule A -- itemize them -- or you can take advantage of the standard deduction. The standard deduction is an amount set forth in the tax law that approximates the average deductible expenses of taxpayers in each filing category (single, joint, etc.). Generally, taxpayers claim whichever figure is higher, their standard deduction or their itemized deductions; the higher the deductions the lower your taxable income.

Depreciation. When you buy an asset for your business or for investment, generally you can deduct the cost of that asset over a period of time known as its "useful life". This gradual deduction is known as depreciation. A discussion of depreciation can be found in the section of Chapter four dealing with the expensing of business assets.

Alternative Minimum Tax (AMT). AMT is a second tax structure designed to insure that taxpayers with lots of clever deductions don't get off scott free. Basically, AMT rules require taxpayers to compute both their regular tax liability and their AMT liability, and then pay whichever is higher. AMT tends to affect only high-income taxpayers, because it includes a substantial "personal exemption" (raised to by OBRA to $33,750 for single filers and $45,000 for joint). It can create real headaches for certain high-income individuals and many corporations. The individual AMT is detailed in the section of Chapter one discussing individual rate increases.

* * * * *

The last Chapter of this book contains a review of the basic tax planning weapons that should be in every taxpayer's arsenal. Throughout earlier chapters, you are encouraged to review specific tax planning strategies in order to minimize the impact of OBRA. These techniques are available to all taxpayers regardless of bracket. Therefore, while you may pick and choose which of the OBRA changes in Chapters one through nine to read in depth, be sure to pay extra attention to Chapter Ten. There should be something in there for everyone, and a way for any reader to lower his or her tax bill.

Many happy returns!!!

CONTENTS

CHAPTER 1

CHANGES AFFECTING INDIVIDUALS

RATES - INDIVIDUAL INCOME TAX RATES

What Was

As of 1 January, 1993, the tax rates imposed on individual taxable income were:

For Single Filers --

If taxable income is:	The tax is:
Not over $22,100	15% of taxable income
Over $22,100 but not over $53,500	$3,315 plus 28% of the amount over $22,100
Over $53,500	$12,107 plus 31% of the amount over $53,500

For Joint Filers or Surviving Spouses --

If taxable income is:	The tax is:
Not over $36,900	15% of taxable income
Over $36,900 but not over $89,150	$5,535 plus 28% of the amount over $36,900
Over $89,150	$20,165 plus 31% of the amount over $89,150

For Married Filing Separately --

If taxable income is:	The tax is.
Not over $18,450	15% of taxable income
Over $18,450 but not over $44,575	$2,767.50 plus 28% of the amount over $18,450
Over $44,575	$10,082 50 plus 31% of the amount over $44,575

For Heads of Household --

If taxable income is:	The tax is:
Not over $29,600	15% of taxable income
Over $29,600 but not over $76,400	$4,440 plus 28% of the amount over $29,600
Over $76,400	$17,544 plus 31% of the amount over $76,400

These rates are indexed each year for inflation. The maximum rate of taxation on capital gains is 28%.

What's New

OBRA 93 builds on the existing tax rate structure by making two significant changes: (1) new higher brackets are added; and, (2) a 10% surtax is added. Moreover, all of these changes were made retroactively to 1 January, 1993. This means income you already have earned may be taxed at higher rates.

New Bracket. OBRA 93 adds a new 36% bracket to the tax rate tables. Accordingly, the additional tax rates now in effect for all of 1993 are as follows:

For Single Filers --

If taxable income is:	The tax is:
Over $115,000	$31,172 plus 36% of the amount over $115,000

For Joint Filers or Surviving Spouses --

If taxable income is:	The tax is:
Over $140,000	$35,928.50 plus 36% of the amount over $140,000

For Married Filing Separately --

If taxable income is:	The tax is:
Over $70,000	$17,962.25 plus 36% of the amount over $70,000

For Heads of Household --

If taxable income is:	The tax is:
Over $127,500	$33,385 plus 36% of the amount over $127,500

The maximum rate of taxation on capital gains remains at 28%.

The new 36% bracket will be adjusted for inflation every year, but starting in 1995.

Surtax. OBRA imposes a 10% surtax on taxable incomes above $250,000. This applies regardless of filing status, except the surtax kicks in for married taxpayers filing separately with taxable incomes above $125,000. The net effect of this change is to create a new fifth bracket at 39.6% (36% x 10% = 3.6%; 3.6% + 36% = 39.6%).

The $250,000 level for imposing the surtax will be indexed for inflation each year, but not until 1995.

What to Do

If you are affected by these rate increases, it is important for you to consider two objectives: (1) shelter current income from taxation; and, (2) make maximum use of those investments favored by the tax law. The discussions below will point you in the right direction to do this, and discuss some other aspects of the rate increases.

Fund Retirement Plans to the Limit. If you are able to defer income through a retirement plan, these new higher rates give you more incentive than ever to do so. Review the section on retirement savings in the last Chapter, paying particular attention to strategies for contributory plans.

Look for Tax-Advantaged Investments. Similarly, tax-advantaged investments have been made even more attractive by the new OBRA rates. Tax-exempt municipal bonds are likely to be favored by many investors who fall within the new 36% and 39.6% tax brackets. Review the section on tax-advantaged investing in the last Chapter of this book to learn how to maximize your investment dollars.

Seek Capital Gains. If you are an investor in the top bracket, you now have a greater incentive to seek investment vehicles which emphasize capital gains (as opposed to interest or dividends). The top income tax rate is 39.6%, but OBRA left the top rate on capital gains at 28%. This differential makes investments that declare capital gains (such as some growth mutual funds) more attractive to taxpayers in the new brackets.

> **Example:** You are in the 36% tax bracket. You are considering investing $10,000 in two different mutual funds. One offers a 10% return, usually in the form of dividends. The other offers a similar return, but through capital gains distributions. If both investments provide a $1,000 pre-tax return, the "dividend fund" will net you only $640 ($1,000 - 36% = $640), whereas the "capital gains fund" will leave you with $720 ($1,000 - 28% = $720). The investment returning capital gains distributions provides a superior after-tax return.

Note that the example above does not consider the state tax consequences of your transaction. If you live in a state that still differentiates between capital gains and ordinary income, the advantage of capital-gains-oriented investing could be even greater. Of course, your investments should also make non-tax sense. Your portfolio should be diversified and consistent with your risk tolerance. Whatever investment you make should be well-researched and highly-rated.

You might also consider the two new special capital gains opportunities created by OBRA. Particularly, investing in "Qualified Small Business Stock" may allow you to lower your capital gains rate to 14%. They are included in the Chapter on changes affecting investors.

Watch Your Withholding. Remember that OBRA's higher rates went into effect last January 1st. If you're going to be in the new higher brackets, you have a withholding problem. If you're an employee, your withholding for at least two-thirds of the year has been based on tables that do not include the new rates. If you're self-employed, at least two (and probably three) of your quarterly estimated payments also were not based on the new rates. You're going to owe money next April 15th.

You may want to adjust for this problem now. Increase your withholdings, or make higher estimated tax payments for the rest of the year, in order to make sure that you won't have to write a big check next April 15th. Even better, start putting the money aside now so you can pay it on the 15th without cramping your finances. This way, you earn interest on the money, not the government. OBRA 93 contains language indicating that you can't be penalized for under-withholding in 1993, as long as the under-withholding is only attributable to the rate hikes. So, while you can wait until the 15th to give the government its extra money, it may pinch your cash flow to do it all at once. Regardless of your method, you should be planning ahead for next April's unpleasantness.

Take Advantage of the Installment Plan. There may be an even better way to pay for your extra 93 taxes, but you have to follow the rules carefully in order to qualify. OBRA contains a provision allowing you to pay part of your taxes in three annual installments. Only those taxes attributable to the rate hikes are eligible for the installment program. You must elect to use the installment method by 15 April, 1994, and make your first payment by then. You can extend your 93 return if you need to, but be certain you have every penny you owe (including the first installment) paid in by the 15th; otherwise, you'll forfeit the option to pay in installments.

If you satisfy these requirements, you can pay the other two installments on 15 April, 1994 and 15 April, 1995 (again, no extensions are allowed for the installment payments). Best of all, no interest accrues on the second and third installments. It's not often the government offers taxpayers an interest free loan, so if you are affected by the new rates and can qualify for the installment plan, don't pass it up!!!

Review Your S Election. OBRA 93 produced an about-face in the logic used by many small business advisors regarding whether their corporate clients should make an election to be treated as an S corporation. If you own an S corporation, review the section on corporate rate hikes in the Chapter on changes affecting businesses to see if your S election still makes good sense.

Shift Income to Lower-Bracket Relatives. If you are in the highest tax brackets, you have a greater incentive than ever to shift income to family members who are taxed at lower rates. There are two important limits on your ability to do this: the Gift Tax rules, and the Kiddie Tax rules. The Gift Tax rules limit to $10,000 per person per year the value of income-producing assets you can transfer to your parents or your children without incurring a Gift Tax. (For a complete discussion of the Gift Tax rules, see the section on estate planning in the last Chapter of this book.) The Kiddie Tax rules limit your ability to take advantage of your children's lower tax rates. (For a complete discussion of the Kiddie Tax rules, see the section on tax bracket arbitrage in the last Chapter of this book.)

If you structure your planning so as not to run afoul of these two limitations, however, you should be able to move some of your income into lower brackets (depending on the size of your family and how well you trust them!!).

RATES - INDIVIDUAL AMT

What Was

Initially, the alternative minimum tax (AMT) rate for 1993 was 24%. To compute AMT, start with your regular taxable income, add back certain "adjustments" and "preference items", and subtract the applicable AMT exemption. The AMT rate is applied to this amount to compute your AMT. You owe the government either your regular tax or your alternative minimum tax, whichever was higher. No part of the AMT is indexed for inflation.

Adjustments and preference items include most itemized deductions and some investment-related deductions. The standard deduction, state and local taxes, miscellaneous itemized deductions, investment interest expense, and extra depreciation you are entitled to claim for regular tax purposes are all examples of adjustments and preferences. A full list of these adjustments and preference items is included on IRS Form 6251, the individual AMT form.

The AMT exemptions are fairly high -- $30,000 for single filers and heads of household, and $40,000 for joint filers ($20,000 if filing separate). Note, however, that you do not claim both the regular tax personal exemption and the AMT personal exemption, but only the latter.

> **Example:** You and your spouse are joint filers with taxable income (before personal exemptions) of $38,000. You itemize your deductions, claiming $6,000 for mortgage interest on your home (including $2,000 in home equity line interest), $3,000 in state income taxes, and $2,000 in charitable contributions. Your regular Federal tax liability is $4,995. Your AMT is $480, computed as follows: $38,000 regular taxable income + $2,000 home equity interest + $2,000 state income tax deduction - $40,000 AMT exemption = $2,000; $2,000 x 24% = $480. You pay regular tax ($4,995), not AMT ($480).

Note that, in this example, your regular tax liability is significantly higher than your AMT liability. This is the case for a clear majority of taxpayers. In practice, AMT is only a concern for taxpayers with very high incomes and very high deductions.

What's New

OBRA made three significant changes to the AMT: (1) increased AMT rates; (2) split the AMT rate structure into two levels; and, (3) raised the AMT exemption.

The new AMT rate structure is as follows: for AMT income up to $175,000, the rate is 26%. For AMT income above this amount, the tax increases to 28%.

The AMT exemptions are $33,750 for single filers and heads of household, and $45,000 for joint filers ($22,500 if filing separately).

What to Do

Don't Panic! First, make sure you are one of those affected by the AMT. Most Americans don't owe any AMT, either because their incomes are well below the AMT exemption amounts or because their regular tax liabilities are higher. Moreover, with the new higher regular tax rates established by OBRA, some people may actually be removed from the AMT rolls.

If you are one of the unfortunate few with AMT woes, OBRA's new higher AMT rates probably have added to your troubles. The AMT is hard to plan around, precisely because it is in some ways targeted at taxpayers who benefit from regular tax planning. If you have serious AMT problems, you probably should be consulting with a tax advisor familiar with the AMT. Nevertheless, here's a few simple options which may be helpful to you (do your math carefully before using any of them, however):

Defer Itemized Deductions. Where possible, charitable, home equity mortgage interest, and medical deductions should be deferred to the next (i.e., non-AMT) tax year if your regular tax bracket will be higher than your AMT bracket in the subsequent year.

Delay Incentive Stock Options. If possible, you should defer the exercise of ISO's until a year when no AMT liability is anticipated.

Accelerate Income. If you clearly are subject to AMT, it may be advantageous to accelerate income to the current tax year. In this way, your marginal income will be taxed at lower AMT rates (26% or 28%) in the earlier year, rather than at 36% or 39.6% in the later year. This option will only make sense if you are in the two highest brackets.

Re-evaluate Investment Decisions. High-income taxpayers certain to be subject to AMT may actually profit from switching out of tax-free investments. Moving to taxable investments can provide a higher after-tax return once the lower AMT rates are applied. Do the math carefully on this one, though.

DEDUCTIONS - MOVING EXPENSES

What Was

When you move from one principal residence to another because of a change in job locations, the tax law allows you to deduct certain reasonable moving expenses if you meet specified tests.

In order for your moving expenses to qualify for deduction, the move itself must meet two tests. First, the move has to be necessitated by a new job or business. If you haven't switched workplaces, your moving expenses are personal and non-deductible. Next, the distance between your old house and new workplace has to be at least 35 miles greater than the distance between your old house and your old workplace.

> **Example:** Before you moved, your commute between your old house and your old workplace was 6 miles. If you had not moved, your commute between your old house and your new workplace would be 47 miles. The difference between these two figures is "at least 35 miles" (in fact, it's 41 (47 - 6 = 41)). You meet the distance requirement for deducting your reasonable moving expenses.

If you meet both tests -- business and distance -- you can deduct the following expenses, but only if you itemize your deductions on Schedule A of Form 1040:

(1) expenses for the transport of your household goods;

(2) travel, meal, and lodging expenses for the transport of you and your family;

(3) travel, meal, and lodging expenses for house-hunting trips;

(4) expenses for meals and temporary lodging for up to 30 days at the "new" location; and,

(5) expenses to sell your old residence and buy a new one, or expenses to settle a lease on your old residence and acquire a new one.

Frequently, employers reimburse employees for these business-related moving expenses. Your employer is required to include the amount of such reimbursements when reporting your income to the IRS on Form W-2.

What's New

OBRA 93 left some of the deductions for business-related moves intact, but trimmed in several targeted areas. It also increased the distance eligibility requirement. These changes are effective 1 January, 1994.

First, the distance requirement was increased from 35 to 50 miles. Thus, in the example above, you would not qualify for the deduction if your move occurs after January 1st, since the distance "differential" is only 41 miles.

Next, after January 1st, the list of eligible deductions shrinks to just the following:

(1) expenses for the transport of your household goods; and,

(2) travel, and lodging expenses (not meals) for the transport of you and your family.

On the positive side, two pro-taxpayer changes were made in this area of the law. First, after January 1st, your employer will no longer be required to include in income on your W-2 any moving-expenses for which it reimburses you. Second, starting in 1994, the expenses will become "above-the-line" deductions if they are not reimbursed. This means you can deduct the two types of expenses listed above whether you itemize your deductions or claim the standard deductions. Again, however, you are only entitled to this above-the-line deduction to the extent your employer has not reimbursed you

$ What to Do

Accelerate Your Move. If you know that you will not meet the new 50 mile distance requirement in 1994, but can meet the 35 mile one in effect until December 31st of this year, try to squeeze your move in before time runs out.

Don't Panic. Although this law change restricts your deductions in some respects, it also has positive components. The rules actually will work to the advantage of some taxpayers. Moving the deduction "above-the-line" will help taxpayers who don't itemize. Eliminating the requirement that your employer include reimbursed moving expenses in your income avoids the possibility of your paying tax on income you didn't actually earn. And, the heart of the moving expense deduction still exists. For most families, the cost of getting themselves and their property from "A" to "B" is usually the lion's share of moving expenses, anyway.

DEDUCTIONS - CHARITABLE CONTRIBUTIONS OF APPRECIATED PROPERTY

What Was

When you make a charitable contribution of property (as opposed to cash), you generally are entitled to claim a deduction for the fair market value of the property you contribute. Your overall deduction for charitable contributions cannot exceed certain percentages of your income for any year -- 20%, 30%, or 50%, depending on the type of property involved and the organization receiving it -- but deductions in excess of the annual limits can be carried forward for up to 5 years.

However, for purposes of computing the individual alternative minimum tax (AMT), the amount by which certain property has appreciated in value is included in the long list of "preference items" which get added back to regular income in determining AMT income.

> **Example:** You donate a painting to a tax-exempt art gallery worth $10,000. You purchased the painting many years earlier for $1,000. Assuming that you do not exceed the overall limit on charitable deductions, you can claim a $10,000 deduction on Schedule A. However, you must include $9,000 ($10,000 - $1,000 = $9,000) as a tax preference item when computing how much, if any, AMT you owe.

Contributions of tangible personal property were exempt from this rule until 30 June, 1992.

What's New

The law requiring appreciation on donated property to be counted as an AMT preference item was repealed retroactively. For tangible personal property, the repeal goes back to contributions after 30 June, 1992. Since this is when the old exception expired, appreciation on tangible personal property was never an AMT preference item. For all other property (e.g., securities, real estate), the repeal is effective for contributions after 31 December, 1992

What To Do

Give, Give, Give! Don't let tax concerns get in the way of your charitable giving anymore. The entire issue was generally only a concern for very wealthy taxpayers who donated very expensive property. Now, it is no longer a concern for anyone. The repeal is intended to encourage charitable giving.

See if a Refund Opportunity Exists. If you paid alternative minimum tax in 1992 and made a charitable contribution between 1 July and 31 December involving tangible personal property that had appreciated in value since you acquired it, review your 1992 return. You may be able to amend it and claim a refund, since the amount of the appreciation on which you paid AMT is no longer taxable. If after reviewing your 1992 return you think you may be entitled to a refund because of this change, consult your tax advisor.

DEDUCTIONS - SUBSTANTIATION OF CHARITABLE CONTRIBUTIONS

What Was

Taxpayers who itemize their deductions are entitled to claim a deduction for the contributions they make to recognized charities. As with any deduction, a taxpayer under audit may be requested to prove that he or she made the charitable contribution for which a deduction was claimed. There is, however, no specific substantiation requirement contained in the tax law -- with one exception. Generally, a cancelled check will suffice.

The exception: if you make charitable contributions of more than $500 in tangible property, you (and sometimes the recipient and/or an appraiser) are required to file a Form 8283, Noncash Charitable Contributions, with your tax return. This allows IRS to verify certain large contributions that in the past have been a source of problems.

What's New

Effective 1 January, 1994, you must obtain written substantiation from any charity to which you donate more than $250 in a single contribution in order to claim a deduction for that contribution.

> **Example 1:** You put $10 in the collection basket at church each week. Even though the total amount you've contributed for the year exceeds $250 ($10 x 52 weeks = $520), you will not need a receipt from the church to claim a deduction.
>
> **Example 2:** On 31 December, 1994, you decide to contribute $300 to your church's building fund. You write two checks for $150 each. You must still obtain a receipt or acknowledgement before you file your 1994 tax return in order to claim the deduction.

As Example 2 suggests, OBRA also contains anti-abuse rules to prevent you from writing multiple checks to get around this rule. The new law does not require any specified form of substantiation, but cancelled checks will no longer be sufficient to claim the deduction. You will need some sort of receipt, acknowledgement, or computer print-out from the charity to be able to claim your deduction.

What to Do

Get Receipts and Save Them. OBRA places the legal burden on you, the donor, to obtain substantiation if you want to claim a deduction for a contribution over $250, and not on the charity to provide it. Of course, most charities are probably gearing up to automatically provide substantiation anyway, since it behooves them to keep contributors happy. Save your acknowledgements, receipts, and print-outs in your tax file. You should keep all supporting documentation, including acknowledgements for charitable contributions in excess of $250, for at least six years after you file your return. (You also should keep a copy of the return itself permanently, but that's not the topic at hand!)

DEDUCTIONS - PARTIAL PHASE-OUT OF ITEMIZED DEDUCTIONS

What Was

Certain high-income taxpayers who itemize their deductions are required to make some complex calculations to reduce the total amount of those deductions. This partial "phase-out" of itemized deductions affects incomes above $108,450 ($54,225 for married filing separately). These figures are indexed annually for inflation. The reduction only applies to certain itemized deductions, sparing others such as medical expenses, investment interest, and casualty losses. In no circumstances can the total hit be more than 80% of total itemized deductions (in reality, it seldom even approaches anything this onerous). Most importantly, the phase-out was supposed to be temporary; 1995 would have been the last year it applied.

What's New

OBRA 93 makes the partial phase-out of itemized deductions permanent.

What to Do

Get Tax-Smart. There really is no way to avoid the partial phase-out of itemized deductions if you fall within its requirements. However, the net effect of this change is to raise your marginal tax rate. Therefore, many of the same strategies recommended for individuals affected by the new higher rates apply to you. Read the section on tax-advantaged investments in the last Chapter of this book. The strategies contained in that section can help you lower your overall tax bite.

If it's any comfort, the net increase in tax rates produced by this provision of the tax law is minimal. For taxpayers in the very highest bracket (39.6%), for example, it produces a maximum increase in marginal rates of about 1.2%.

EXEMPTIONS - PHASE-OUT OF PERSONAL EXEMPTIONS

What Was

High-income taxpayers are required to reduce or even eliminate the personal exemptions claimed on their tax returns. This gradual "phase-out" of personal exemptions affects single taxpayers with income above $108,450, joint filers with income above $162,700 ($81,350 if filing separately), and heads of household with incomes above $135,600. These figures are indexed annually for inflation. Because of the way the phase-out computation works, the exemptions are completely phased out at incomes exceeding the base amounts just listed by more than $122,500.

> **Example:** A single filer with income of $230,951 would not be entitled to claim his personal exemption ($108,450 + $122,500 = $230,950). The personal exemption, which is also indexed for inflation, is worth $2,350 in 1993.

The phase-out was supposed to be temporary; 1996 would have been the last year it applied.

What's New

OBRA makes the personal exemption phase-out permanent.

What to Do

Focus on the Big Picture. There really is no way to avoid the phase-out of personal exemptions if your income is above its limits. However, the net effect of this change is to raise your marginal tax rate. Therefore, many of the same strategies recommended for individuals affected by the new higher rates apply to you. Read the section on tax-advantaged investments in the last Chapter of this book. The strategies there can help you lower your overall tax bite.

The net increase in tax rates produced by this provision of the law is negligible. For taxpayers in the very highest bracket (39.6%), for example, it produces a maximum increase in marginal rates of between two-thirds and three-quarters of one percentage point.

LOSSES - PRINCIPAL RESIDENCES IN DISASTER AREAS

What Was

If your home is damaged or destroyed by a natural disaster -- called an "involuntary conversion" in tax lingo -- and the President declares a disaster area there, the tax law provides you with some special relief. Otherwise, any insurance proceeds you receive to compensate you for your loss could possibly turn your misfortune into a taxable transaction with capital gains!! The involuntary conversion rules are designed to soften this blow. Consider the following simplified example:

> **Example:** You purchased your home five years ago for $100,000, and insure it for its replacement cost. Your home is completely destroyed by a tornado, and the President declares the county in which you live a disaster area. The insurance company pays you $125,000 (the fair market value) for your loss. This involuntary conversion results in a $25,000 capital gain to you ($125,000 - $100,000 = $25,000).

There are actually a few more technical in's and out's to the involuntary conversion of a primary residence, but this gives you the sense of how the law works.

The law does give you time to replace or re-build your residence and avoid the tax. Prior to OBRA, the general rule was that you had until the end of the second year after you receive your insurance proceeds to replace the home you lost. (If you receive your proceeds in installments, generally the clock starts ticking after the amount of proceeds you've received exceeds what you paid for your old house.) The cost of your replaced or re-built residence must exceed the amount of insurance proceeds you receive, however.

> **Example:** In the example above, assume you purchased a new home in the same year you lost your old one, paying $120,000. You now have a taxable gain of only $5,000 ($125,000 - $120,000 = $5,000)

The old law also distinguished between insurance proceeds you received for replacement of your residence and those you received for replacement of its contents. That is, you were required to spend real estate insurance proceeds to purchase new real estate, and contents proceeds for new contents. This created a problem for people who live in highly-appreciated real estate. They wanted -- or needed -- to apply some of the insurance proceeds received for their destroyed contents to reconstruction of the house itself, in order to be able to afford to re-build. While the tax law didn't stop them from doing this, of course, it also didn't let them count insurance proceeds from contents towards the purchase price of their replacement residence. This made it difficult for them to satisfy all the involuntary conversion rules and avoid paying tax.

What's New

OBRA made three very important changes for people whose homes are destroyed in Federally-declared disasters.

First, it increases the replacement period from two to four years.

Next, the law no longer requires taxpayers to distinguish between insurance reimbursements for contents and those for the house itself.

Finally, the involuntary conversion rules don't apply to insurance proceeds for "unscheduled" property. This is personal property for which you do not have scheduled -- i.e., itemized -- insurance coverage. This means affected taxpayers won't be required to recognize gain on insurance proceeds received for such property.

The provisions are effective for disasters declared after 31 August, 1991 and for tax years ending after that date.

What to Do

Build, Build, Build. These are pro-taxpayer changes; use them to your advantage! The expanded replacement period can be a big help for people who choose to re-build. Negotiating with insurance claims adjusters, obtaining building permits, and dealing with a scarcity of contractors or materials in an area with widespread damage can make it difficult to get the job done within the old time limit. Eliminating the distinction in the application of insurance proceeds (contents vs. dwelling) means you can use that money to rebuild your life as you see fit, without having to worry about possible adverse tax consequences. As long as you spend all of your insurance proceeds, you will not be required to pay tax on any "involuntary conversion gain".

Watch for a Potential Refund Opportunity. The rule applies to disasters declared after 31 August 1991 and for tax years ending after that date. Thus, if you were the victim of a disaster declared after 31 August, and for some reason have already reported an involuntary conversion gain on a 1991 or 1992 tax return, you have two possible refund opportunities. First, if your gain arose because you were caught up in the old contents-versus-dwelling segregation requirements, or because you were required to report gain on the conversion of unscheduled property, you may be eligible to amend your return and lower or eliminate your gain. This would generate a refund.

Next, if you paid tax on an involuntary conversion gain because you did not replace your residence with one of equal or greater value, you now have two more years to try to do so. Similarly, you now have two more years to make the capital improvements that can increase the value of your replacement residence, thereby reducing or eliminating your gain. If you make these expenditures within the new timeframes, it will create another potential refund opportunity.

These refund opportunities probably only exist for a handful of people nationwide, but if you think you might be one of them, consult your tax advisor for details.

ESTIMATED TAX PAYMENTS - COMPUTATIONS

What Was

Certain taxpayers are required to make quarterly estimated tax payments. Usually, they are either self-employed people, retirees, or individuals who for some other reason cannot satisfy their "pay-as-you-go" tax obligations through wage withholding.

The tax law imposes penalties on individuals who are required to make estimated tax payments but fail to do so. Since it's sometimes hard to estimate what your future tax liability is going to be, the law gives individual taxpayers two "safe harbors" in order to avoid penalties. If you meet either one, penalties for failing to make estimated tax payments usually cannot be assessed against you.

The first safe harbor requires you to pay in an amount equal to 90% of the current year's actual tax liability, usually in quarterly installments. The second one requires you to pay in 100% of the previous year's total tax liability, always in equal quarterly installments. Since it is so hard to estimate your current year's taxes, the first safe harbor isn't really that safe. That's why most people who have to make estimated tax payments rely on the second.

However, the second safe harbor generally is not available to any taxpayer with income over $75,000 if that income also represents an increase of more than $40,000 over the prior year. These taxpayers are required to meet the first safe harbor. This has proven impossible for some taxpayers, especially small business owners and investors. They simply cannot find a way to satisfy their obligations without incurring a penalty.

What's New

Under OBRA, taxpayers previously denied the "100%-of-prior-year's-tax" safe harbor because of their high incomes have a new way to avoid estimated tax penalties. Effective 1 January, 1994, taxpayers with income of $150,000 or less can avoid estimated tax penalties by paying 100% of the prior year's total tax liability in four equal quarterly installments (the current rule). Taxpayers with incomes above $150,000 can avoid penalties by paying 110% of the prior year's tax in four equal quarterly installments. Of course, the "90%-of-current-year's tax" safe harbor is still available for those who think they can satisfy it.

What to Do

Sleep Easy. If you were one of the high-income taxpayers affected by the tax trap under the old law, pay in 110% of last year's total tax and enjoy this pro-taxpayer simplification.

CREDITS - EARNED INCOME TAX CREDIT

What Was

The tax law offers a credit to low-income working parents who meet certain conditions. The credit, known as the earned income tax credit (EITC), can be used to offset other taxes or even to generate a tax refund. The EITC consists of three parts: (1) a basic credit; (2) a health insurance credit; and, (3) a supplemental young child credit.

The credit in 1993 is 18.5% of the first $7,750 of earned income. The credit starts to phase out when income exceeds $12,200, and is completely eliminated when income exceeds $23,000. The 18.5% is increased to 19.5% for workers with more than one child. The maximum credit in 1993 therefore is $1,434 ($1,511 if you have more than one child). The EITC is indexed annually for inflation.

Taxpayers claiming the EITC who expect a refund because of it are eligible to receive EITC payments in advance of filing their returns, within limits. Such advance payments are arranged through one's employer after filing a certificate of eligibility.

Computing the basic credit and the two supplemental credits can be very complicated. Ironically, this complexity has a disproportionate impact on exactly the people the EITC seeks to help.

What's New

Starting in 1994, the credit will be expanded and simplified. The expansion means that more people will qualify for the credit, and the simplification means that it will be easier for those who do qualify to claim it.

If you are a worker with one child, the credit in 1994 will be increased to 26.3% of the first $7,750 in earned income. The maximum credit in 1994 therefore will be $2,038 ($7,750 x 26.3% = $2,038). The credit will be phased-out by 15.98% of earned income exceeding $11,000, and therefore will be completely eliminated when income reaches $23,753 ($2,038/15.98% = $12,753; $12,753 +

$11,000 = $23,753). In 1995, the credit will increase from 26.3% to 34% but the base amount will decrease from $7,750 to $6,000.

> **Example:** In 1994, you have one child and earn $14,000. You are entitled to an EITC of $1,559, computed as follows: $14,000 - $11,000 = $3,000; $3,000 x 15.98% = $479; $2,038 - $479 = $1,559.

If you are a worker with more than one child, the credit in 1994 will be increased to 30% of the first $8,425 in earned income. The maximum credit in 1994 therefore will be $2,527 ($8,425 x 30% = $2,527). The credit will be phased-out by 17.68% of income exceeding $11,000, and therefore will be completely eliminated when income reaches $25,293 ($2,527/17.68% = $14,293; $14,293 + $11,000 = $25,293). In 1995, the credit will increase from 30% to 36%, and the phase-out percentage will increase from 17.68% to 20.22%. From 1996 on, the credit will be 40% and the phase-out percentage 21.06%.

> **Example 1:** Same facts as in the example above, but you have two children. You are entitled to an EITC of $1,997, computed as follows: $14,000 - $11,000 = $3,000; $3,000 x 17.68% = $530; $2,527 - $530 = $1,997.

> **Example 2:** Same facts as in the previous example, but it is now 1995 and the maximum credit is $3,033 ($8,425 x 36% = $3,033). You are now entitled to an EITC of $2,426, computed as follows: $14,000 - $11,000 = $3,000; $3,000 x 20.22% = $607; $3,033 - $607 = $2,426.

If you are a worker with no children, the new EITC creates for the first time a credit which may be available to you. The credit will be 7.65% of the first $4,000 in income. The credit will begin to phase-out when income exceeds $5,000, and will be completely eliminated above $9,000. The maximum credit in 1994 is $306. You must be between the ages of 25 and 65 to claim this credit.

The EITC will continue to be indexed annually for inflation

beginning in 1995. Eligible employees may continue to claim advance EITC payments through their employers. Finally, the two supplemental credits are repealed beginning in 1994.

What to Do

Take Credit Where Credit Is Due. Do the math and see if you qualify for the EITC. If you do, don't be ashamed to claim it; it's only there to help you. If you need assistance computing your credit during tax season, your local IRS office can direct you to a volunteer program in your area. Take advantage of the help and the credit. If you think you may qualify for advance EITC payments, contact your personnel office.

CHAPTER 2

CHANGES AFFECTING EMPLOYERS AND EMPLOYEES

FRINGE BENEFITS - EMPLOYER-PROVIDED EDUCATION ASSISTANCE

What Was

Unless there's a specific exception in the tax law, anything of value given to an employee by an employer is considered income. For example, without a specific exemption, the cost of the group term life insurance or group medical insurance offered as fringe benefits by many employers would be includible as part of an employee's income. Fortunately, there is such an exception for these items, so they're not includible in an employee's income.

Most of these exceptions in the law are permanent; a few have expiration dates. One provision that expired on 30 June, 1992 related to tuition reimbursement programs offered by employers. Until that date, employees could receive up to $5,250 annually in educational assistance without having any of it included in income.

What's New

OBRA 93 extended the exclusion from 1 July, 1992 to 31 December, 1994.

What to Do

Hit the Books! Take advantage of this pro-taxpayer change (and your employer's generosity) to brush up on your career or other skills before the provision expires again.

Look for a Refund Opportunity. If you received tuition reimbursement from your employer in the second half of 1992, it was probably included in your income on Form W-2 (some employers also report this information in Box 18 of the W-2; look there first). This means you paid tax on the amount of the reimbursement, but OBRA 93 now says you didn't have to. If you are in this situation, you are eligible for a refund. You can claim a refund of income taxes paid on affected tuition reimbursements by filing an amended return with IRS, but first they must get a corrected W-2 (Form W-2c) from their employers. You also can ask your employer to reimburse Social Security taxes paid on affected tuition assistance; speak to your personnel office for details. (Your employer will then claim a credit on its quarterly payroll tax form (Form 941) for the amount it refunds you.) If you can't get a refund of Social Security taxes from your employer, consult your local IRS office about how to file a Form 843, Claim for Refund.

If you are an employer, you may claim a refund for Social Security and unemployment taxes they paid on affected tuition reimbursements; consult your Circular E for details.

PENSIONS - AMOUNT OF COMPENSATION USED TO COMPUTE BENEFITS

What Was

The tax law imposes limits on the amount of an employee's income that retirement plans can take into account when calculating contributions or benefits for that employee in any given year. The limit, which is indexed for inflation, is $235,840 for 1993. Thus, high wage-earners can only have contributions to pension plans made on their behalf with respect to their first $235,840 in income.

> **Example:** You earn $300,000 per year. Your employer provides a defined contribution pension plan in which a flat 6% of salary is contributed on each employee's behalf. Your employer can only contribute $14,150.40 to the plan on your behalf in 1993 ($235,840 x 6% = $14,150.40). Without this limitation, your employer would be able to contribute $18,000 on your behalf in 1993 ($300,000 x 6% = $18,000).

What's New

OBRA 93 lowers the $235,840 limit to $150,000, effective 1 January, 1994. The limit will continue to be adjusted for inflation, but only in $10,000 increments.

> **Example:** In the example above, assuming your salary does not change, your employer will only be able to contribute $9,000 to your retirement plan on your behalf in 1994 ($150,000 x 6% = $9,000).

What to Do

Consider Non-qualified Plans. Since the restriction discussed above only applies to plans that qualify for favorable treatment under the tax law, employers and key employees may want to take a look at any of the several available non-qualified plans. These include deferred compensation arrangements, salary continuation plans, "top-hat" plans, and rabbi trusts. Although a discussion of the mechanics of these various plans is beyond the scope of this book, a tax or pension advisor should be able to help you choose and implement a plan that will meet your needs. Keep in mind that the tax consequences to the employer and the employee can vary in these plans. Unless the plan is carefully structured, it can result in the immediate recognition of income by the employee. This, of course, runs contrary to the main goal of deferring compensation.

Consider Excess Benefit Plans. An excess benefit plan is a particular type of non-qualified plan which is designed to counter precisely the limits modified by OBRA. The plan, using one of the non-qualified deferral mechanisms discussed above, provides a benefit equal to the amount "disallowed" under the qualified plan.

> **Example:** In the last example above, if you are covered by an excess benefit plan, the $9,000 the tax law does not allow your employer to contribute to its qualified plan on your behalf in 1994 would be contributed to a non-qualified deferred compensation arrangement ($18,000 - $9,000 = $9,000).

As with other non-qualified plans, excess benefit plans may or may not result in the immediate recognition of income by the employee, depending on how they are structured. It therefore again is advisable to consult with an expert when selecting and implementing an excess benefit plan.

Watch Your 401(k). If you are covered by a 401(k) plan, this change in the law may have the ultimate effect of limiting the amount you can defer under the plan. The new law is going to make more 401(k) plans "top heavy" and this means they will be required to trim back the contributions made by their "highly compensated employees". If you're an affected employee, there's no way to avoid the problem, but at least be aware of it. If you are able to determine in advance what your contribution limits will be, you may wish to adjust your deferral percentage in order to maintain a more even cash flow throughout the year.

TAX WITHHOLDING - SUPPLEMENTAL WAGE PAYMENTS

What Was

The tax law refers to certain forms of compensation, such as bonuses, commissions, and the exercise of stock options as "supplemental wages". The law requires employers to withhold income taxes on these payments. (It also requires FICA withholding, but that's not a concern here). Employers can either use special withholding tables to compute the proper amount to withhold or they can withhold tax at a flat 20%.

What's New

Effective 1 January, 1994, the optional supplemental withholding rate is increased from 20% to 28%.

$ What to Do

Employees - Watch Your Withholding. Congress says this change is intended to make the rate of withholding more closely match the actual amount of taxes that will be owed on the payments in question. The flat rate on supplemental wages is optional, but many employers use it because it allows them to by-pass time-consuming computations.

However, a flat rate will affect different people in different ways. If the flat 28% leaves you over-withheld and you can't convince your employer not to use it, you may be stuck. Consider decreasing the amount withheld from your regular pay in order to compensate for the extra being taken out from your commissions or bonuses. There's no incentive for giving the government an interest free loan in the form of your excess withholding.

Some people, however, may find themselves under-withheld at the 28% level. With upper brackets now at 39.6%, supplemental wage withholding at the rate of 28% may be insufficient for high-income earners. If you think this applies to you, re-compute your W-4 to see if you need additional withholding from your regular pay to make up the shortfall and avoid penalties.

SOCIAL SECURITY TAXES - MEDICARE WAGE BASE CAP

What Was

All workers (and their employers) must pay Social Security taxes on their wages. The tax for each is 7.65%. A self-employed person pays both the employer and employee share of these taxes (although some adjustments and deductions are allowed to compensate somewhat for this burden).

Social Security taxes consist of two components - OASDI (Old Age, Survivors, and Disability Insurance) and Medicare. OASDI accounts for 6.2% of the 7.65% tax, and Medicare for the other 1.45% (6.2% + 1.45% = 7.65%).

The tax is not imposed on an unlimited amount of income, however. For OASDI, the tax stops after wages exceed $57,600 in 1993 (indexed annually for inflation). The Medicare tax applies to the first $135,000 in wages in 1993 (also indexed).

Note that, if you switch jobs during the year, your new employer must "re-set the clock" and start collecting the taxes until your new salary exceeds the wage base. If you end up having too much Social Security tax withheld because of a job change, you can claim a credit for the excess when you file your tax return.

What's New

Effective 1 January, 1994, the wage base on the Medicare portion of Social Security taxes will be eliminated. This means that you and your employer will be required to pay Medicare taxes (1.45% each) on all your wages, regardless of how high they are. If you are self-employed, the 2.9% tax (1.45% x 2 = 2.9%) likewise will be imposed on all of your net business income.

What to Do

Look for Savings Elsewhere. If your income exceeds $135,000, this is essentially a tax rate increase for you. Therefore, many of the suggestions offered to those individuals affected by the new higher rates apply to you. Again, maximizing retirement plan contributions and seeking tax-favored investment income can help here. Besides, if you're an employee, it's hard to do too much planning around a tax rate increase of 1.45% on your income in excess of $135,000.

If you're a high-income self-employed person, however, you're rate increase is effectively going to be 2.9%. All other things being equal (and you should make sure they are), you may want to consider trying to shift some income from 1994 into 1993 if you're going to be affected by these higher Medicare taxes.

SOCIAL SECURITY TAXES - EMPLOYER CREDIT FOR TAXES PAID ON TIPS

What Was

For purposes of computing Social Security (FICA) taxes, employers are treated as the payors of any tip income received by their employees. Thus, the employer is required to pay its share -- 7.65% -- of the FICA tax on its employees' tip income.

What's New

Effective 1 January, 1994, food and beverage establishments where tipping is "customary" will be eligible to claim a credit against their tax liability for a portion of the FICA they pay on their employees' tips. The credit, while unlimited in dollar amount, is only available for that portion of FICA paid on tips in excess of the Federal minimum wage.

> **Example:** It is 1994. You own a restaurant. You pay your employees $3.00 per hour, but they earn $10.00 per hour after tips. Your city imposes a minimum wage of $5.00 per hour; the Federal minimum wage is $4.25 per hour. For simplicity's sake assume your employees work a standard 2,080 hour year (40 hours/week x 52 weeks = 2,080). Thus, your employees' annual salaries are $20,800, on which you as their employer pay $1,591.20 in FICA tax ($20,800 x 7.65% = $1,591.20). You are entitled to claim a credit against your total tax liability of $914.94 for each employee, computed thus: difference between Federal minimum wage and hourly salary x hours worked/year x FICA rate = $5.75 x 2,080 x 7.65% = $914.94. Also note that you are allowed to claim a business deduction of $676.26 per employee ($1,591.20 - $914.94 = $676.26), which represents the FICA on their salary up to the Federal minimum wage.

Notice in this example that your city's minimum wage was ignored. That's because the credit applies with regard to the Federal minimum wage. If your state, city, or county has a higher minimum wage, use the Federal one for this purpose (i.e., $4.25 per hour).

A final warning: the current practice is for employers to claim all of the FICA they pay as a business deduction. Once this change becomes effective, an employer won't be entitled to also take a deduction for any FICA taxes on which it chooses to claim this new credit. In the example above, FICA taxes on tips above the Federal minimum wage were used to claim the new credit, while FICA on tips below it were claimed as a deduction.

What to Do

Eat, Drink, and Be Merry! This change is a win for taxpayers! As a general rule, credits are always better than deductions. That's because, deductions only reduce income, while credits provide a dollar-for-dollar reduction on the tax you owe. This change was included in OBRA to placate the hospitality industry, which was concerned about the reduction in the business meals deduction (discussed elsewhere in this book).

CHAPTER 3

CHANGES AFFECTING RETIREES

SOCIAL SECURITY - TAXATION OF BENEFITS

What Was

Taxpayers with "provisional income" above specified thresholds are required to pay income tax on the lower of: (1) 50% of their annual Social Security benefits; or, (2) 50% of the amount by which their provisional income exceeds a specified threshold. The threshold kicks in for single taxpayers with provisional income above $25,000, for joint filers with provisional income above $32,000, and for married taxpayers filing separately with provisional income above $0.

Provisional income generally consists of the following: (1) all taxable sources of income other than Social Security benefits; (2) tax exempt interest income; (3) certain foreign income; and, (4) 50% of all Social Security benefits received.

> **Example:** You are a single taxpayer, age 67. You receive the following annual income: $14,000 in a taxable pension, $6,000 in taxable dividends, $5,000 in taxable interest income, $10,000 in Social Security benefits, and $6,000 in tax-exempt interest income. $5,000 of your Social Security benefits is taxable, as computed on page 44.

What's New

OBRA 93 imposes a new "second tier" of taxation on the benefits of certain Social Security recipients. The rules described above continue to apply to taxpayers not affected by the changes described here.

OBRA establishes new thresholds on which higher portions of either Social Security or excess provisional income are subject to tax. The new thresholds are $34,000 for single filers, and $44,000 for joint filers. The new inclusion percentage is 85%, but a special adjustment allows you to apply the 50% inclusion rate on includible income above the old thresholds but below the new ones. Thus, for provisional incomes above the new threshold, you are required to pay taxes on the lesser of: (1) 85% of your Social Security benefits; or (2) 85% of provisional income in excess of the new thresholds, plus the lesser of either: (a) the inclusion amount as calculated under the old law or (b) $4,500 ($6,000 for joint filers).

> **Example:** Assume the same facts as above, but it is after the law change has become effective. You are affected by the new second tier, and $5,200 of your Social Security benefits is now taxable, as computed on page 45.

In this example, the amount of your Social Security benefits subject to income tax has increased from $5,000 under the old law to $6,200 under the new law.

If you are married filing a separate return and affected by this new second tier of taxation, you include in income the lesser of 85% of social security benefits or 85% of provisional income. This is because your threshold under the new rules continues to be $0.

In the end, a maximum of 85% of Social Security benefits can be subject to income tax. This figure is intended to approximate the percentage of other retirement plan payments usually subject to tax.

This new second tier is effective for benefits received beginning in 1994.

What to Do

Review Your Overall Strategies. There really is no way to avoid the new 85% rule if you fall within its requirements. However, the net effect of this change is to raise your marginal tax rate. Therefore, many of the same strategies recommended for individuals affected by the new higher rates apply to you. Read the section on tax-advantaged investments in the last Chapter of this book. The strategies contained in that section can help you lower your overall tax bite. Keep in mind, however, that tax-exempt interest income is taken into account when computing your "provisional income".

If it's any consolation, it has been estimated that only 13% of Social Security recipients will be affected by this change.

Taxability of Social Security Benefits Before OBRA:

(A)	Compute Provisional Income:	
(1)	pension	$14,000
	dividends	6,000
	taxable interest	5,000
(2)	tax-exempt interest	6,000
(3)	50% of Social Security	5,000
	Provisional Income:	$36,000
(B)	Compute 50% of Excess Provisional Income:	
	Provisional Income:	$36,000
	- Applicable Threshold:	(25,000)
	Excess Provisional Income:	$11,000
	x 50%:	$ 5,500
(C)	Compute 50% of Social Security Benefits:	
	Social Security Benefits	$10,000
	x 50%:	$ 5,000
(D)	Include Lesser of Result in (B) or (C) in Income.	

Taxability of Social Security Benefits After OBRA:

(A)	Compute Provisional Income:	
(1)	pension	$14,000
	dividends	6,000
	taxable interest	5,000
(2)	tax-exempt interest	6,000
(3)	50% of Social Security	5,000
	Provisional Income:	$36,000
(B)	Compute Includible Provisional Income:	
	Provisional Income:	$36,000
	- Applicable Threshold:	(54,000)
	Excess Provisional Income:	$ 2,000
	x 85%:	$ 1,700
	+ Lesser of inclusion amount under old law (here, $5,000) or $4,500:	$ 4,500
	Includible Provisional Income:	$ 6,200
(C)	Compute 85% of Social Security Benefits:	
	Social Security Benefits	$10,000
	x 85%:	$ 8,500
(D)	Include Lesser of Result in (B) or (C) in Income	

MEDICAID - ASSET TRANSFERS TO QUALIFY FOR COVERAGE

What Was

In order to qualify for Medicaid, an individual must be of limited financial means. When someone applies for Medicaid's long-term care coverage, state authorities must review the person's financial background to see if any assets were transferred to friends and family members as gifts within 30 months of the application. If the state authorities find evidence of such gifts, eligibility for long-term care under Medicaid is delayed for as long as those assets would have funded such long-term care.

This rule has resulted in some senior citizens setting up Medicaid Qualifying Trusts in order to protect their assets while still qualifying for Medicaid coverage. These trusts allow seniors to put their assets outside of Medicaid's reach while still enjoying the benefit of receiving some income from them. Even so, such trusts must be established at least 30 months before an individual applies for Medicaid coverage. Many families have concluded that the prohibitive cost of long-term care makes such arrangements the only viable means of protecting a lifetime of savings.

What's New

Effective 1 October, 1993, OBRA increases the 30 month "waiting period" to 36 months, and to as long as five years in some circumstances.

What to Do

Plan Early. If you are a senior, or have parents who are seniors, it is not too early to begin planning for long-term care. Even people with considerable assets find that long-term care quickly care consumes those assets. Medicaid Qualifying Trusts are a viable option in planning for long-term care, but this change requires you to plan early. Consult an attorney or financial planner with experience in this area for advice on how to proceed.

CHAPTER 4

CHANGES AFFECTING BUSINESSES

RATES - CORPORATE TAX RATES

What Was

Prior to the passage of OBRA 93, the tax rate structure for regular C corporations (i.e., those that were not personal service corporations and did not make a Subchapter S election) was as follows:

If taxable income is:	The tax is:
Not over $50,000	15% of taxable income
Over $50,000 but not over $75,000	$7,500 plus 25% of the amount over $50,000
Over $75,000	$13,750 plus 34% of the amount over $75,000

These tables are not indexed for inflation each year as the individual and trust income tax tables are. If a corporation has taxable income greater than $100,000, then the tax computation in the table above changes in order to eliminate the beneficial effect of the 15% and 25% brackets. Thus, a corporation with taxable income in excess of $335,000 pays income tax at a flat rate of 34%. Personal service corporations (generally corporations formed by doctors, lawyers, accountants, architects and other professionals) are taxed at a flat rate of 34%.

Note that the maximum 28% rate on capital gains available to individuals and trusts does not apply to the capital gains of corporations. Thus, for corporations, capital gains are taxed at the same rates as ordinary income.

What's New

OBRA 93 adds a new top rate of 35% for certain "high-income" corporations. The rate applies to taxable incomes in excess of $10 million. As with the old rate structure, the benefit of the lower brackets is phased-out. The phase-out starts at taxable incomes of $15 million, and corporations with taxable income in excess of $18,333,333 will pay tax at a flat rate of 35%. Capital gains are still taxed the same as ordinary income for corporations, which means they could be subject to a rate as high as 35%. The flat rate imposed on personal service corporations also increases to 35%.

To make matters more difficult, these new rates are effective retroactively -- to 1 January, 1993. Although the law waives any penalties for under-payment of estimates if they're attributable to the law change, affected corporations must pay the new taxes by the return's due date. The three-year installment payment option offered to individuals affected by retroactive rate increases is not available to corporations.

If your corporation operates on a fiscal year instead of a calendar year, it will pay taxes at a blended rate for the year affected by the change. Your corporation's tax is computed by applying both the old and new rate tables to its taxable income, and then taking a weighted average of those two figures based on the number of days in its fiscal year before and after 1 January.

Because of the retroactive effective date on this increase, it is possible for corporations whose 1993 fiscal year has already closed to owe additional tax.

> **Example:** Your corporation's fiscal year ends March 31st. For the fiscal year ended 31 March, 1993, your corporation owes additional tax if its taxable income is over $10 million.

What to Do

Review the S Option. These changes apply only to C corporations; Since S corporations are "pass-through" entities, they are affected by the increase in individual tax rates. For pass-through entities, the items of income, deduction, gain or loss, and credit attributable to an S corporation flow through to the corporation's shareholders, usually in proportion to their interests in the corporation. This means that the S corporation's net income is taxed only once. C corporations, by contrast, usually have their net income taxed twice: once when it is earned by the corporation, and a second time when it is distributed to shareholders in the form of taxable dividends.

Since the Tax Reform Act of 1986 became effective, the top corporate rate has been higher than the top individual rate. This prompted many corporations to elect S status, both to avoid double taxation and to take advantage of the lower individual rates. Now, however, with top corporate rates lower than top individual rates, some corporate owners may actually benefit from C status.

Of course, such a switch isn't for everyone; in fact, it's not even for everyone hit by the new higher rates. Marginal rates are not the only factor involved in the C-versus-S decision-making process. Double taxation on the distributed income of C corporations must weigh into the process, as well as a tricky set of rules applicable to S corporations who switched from C status with appreciated assets. These "built-in gain" rules, as well as all the other pros and cons of switching from S back to C status, can be explained by your tax advisor. You would be foolish to make such a change without consulting him or her first. Among other things, the law imposes limits on your ability to switch from S back to C status, and you could be forced to live with a mistake for many years.

Watch Your Estimated Tax Payments. Remember that OBRA's higher rates went into effect last January 1st. If your corporation's going to be in these new higher brackets, it has an estimated tax payment problem. At least two (and probably three) of its quarterly estimated payments were not based on the new rates. It's going to owe money when it files its next return.

You may want to adjust for this problem now. Make higher estimated tax payments for the rest of the year, in order to make sure that you won't have to write a big check next March 15th (or whenever your return is due if your corporation isn't on a calendar year). Even better, start putting the money aside now so you can pay it on the 15th without cramping your company's finances. This way, your business earns interest on the money, not the government. OBRA 93 contains language indicating that you can't be penalized for under-payment of estimated taxes in 1993, as long as the under-payment is only attributable to the rate hikes. Regardless of your method, your corporation should be planning ahead for next year's unpleasantness.

DEDUCTIONS - EXPENSING OF SMALL BUSINESS ASSETS

What Was

If you purchase an asset for use in your trade or business, or for investment purposes, you are allowed to claim a deduction for the amount you paid. The deduction claimed is called depreciation, and it is spread out over a period of time referred to as the asset's "useful life". In very limited circumstances, the assets you are required to purchase in order to perform your work as an employee can qualify for the depreciation deduction.

Useful lives vary based on the type of asset. Land, for example, can't be depreciated at all, because its useful life is indefinite. Computers get depreciated over five years, and office furniture over seven.

A very complex and intricate body of law has evolved around the depreciation deduction, and entire volumes have been written about the subject. One of the major goals in depreciation planning is to write assets off over the shortest possible period of time. The less time it takes to depreciate an asset,the larger and quicker the deductions.

In order to assist small businesses in acquiring capital assets, the tax law contains a special provision known commonly as Section 179. Section 179 allows certain small businesses to immediately write-off up to $10,000 of depreciable assets. In order to qualify, the total amount of assets purchased by the business in one year cannot exceed $200,000. Above this amount, the value of the write-off is phased out over a $10,000 range; it is completely gone by $210,000. By limiting the ability to "expense" assets all at once to businesses who purchase under $200,000 worth of equipment, the law in effect limits the availability of this deduction to small businesses. Larger firms routinely place in service assets worth much more than $200,000.

Example: You run a small business. You purchase for $5,000 a new computer to be used exclusively for business purposes. This is the only asset you buy for the year. As was mentioned above, computers have a useful life of 5 years. If you claimed the normal depreciation deduction for a computer, you would be allowed to deduct $1,000 for the current year ($5,000/5 = $1,000). (Actually, because the rules are so complicated your deduction would somewhat vary from this amount depending on the month in which you purchased it. This figure, however, is valid for comparison purposes). However, if you claimed a Section 179 deduction for the computer, you could deduct the entire $5,000 all at once. If you are in the 28% bracket, this additional $4,000 deduction would save you an extra $1,120 in taxes ($4,000 x 28% = $1,120). Further, if you are self-employed, the additional deduction would reduce by $4,000 the amount of your income subject to Social Security taxes.

What's New

OBRA 93 increases the limit on Section 179 expensing from $10,000 to $17,500, effective for tax years beginning after 1992.

What to Do

Get Out There and Stimulate. Congress included this provision in an attempt to encourage business investment, hoping that it would stimulate the economy by doing so. Use this pro-taxpayer change to your business' advantage.

Watch Your Timing. If you own a business that runs on a fiscal year instead of a calendar year, be careful when you make your new purchases. The Section 179 limit increases for tax years beginning after 1992. If your fiscal year ends on November 30th, for example, wait until December 1st to make your purchases. By 1 January, 1994, the change will be effective for all taxpayers.

DEDUCTIONS - AMORTIZATION OF ACQUIRED INTANGIBLE ASSETS

What Was

When two parties agree to the sale of a going business, the purchase price reflects the parties estimation of the business' value (theoretically). That value can be said to consist of two components: the value of the businesses' physical assets, and the value of its intangible assets.

Physical assets are easy to identify and assign a value to, but intangible assets are more difficult to ascertain. They can include just about any intangible aspect of the business the parties identify. Consider some common examples:

> **Example 1:** You are a dentist. You negotiate the purchase of a going dental practice from another dentist who plans to retire. You have agreed to purchase many physical assets, including dental equipment, office equipment, and perhaps even a building itself. You also have agreed to purchase several intangible assets, including the selling dentist's patient list, the computer software used to generate client bills, and the "goodwill" (i.e., reputation) his or her practice has generated over the years.

> **Example 2:** You have just negotiated a contract to purchase a small printing business. It is part of a national franchise. As part of the purchase agreement, the seller will promise to stay out of the printing business for three years. You are purchasing such physical assets as printing equipment and supplies, office equipment, and perhaps the actual building that houses the operation. You are also purchasing several intangible assets, including the seller's customer list, his or her goodwill, his or her agreement with the national franchisor, and the "covenant not to compete" with you.

It is important to a buyer to be able to identify and value as many legitimate intangible assets in a purchase as possible. Here's why: after the business is purchased, the buyer is allowed to begin writing off the assets he or she has acquired. Physical assets are depreciated over their useful life based on their fair market value. Intangible assets similarly are "amortized" over their useful life based on their value. However, if an asset does not have a useful life, it cannot be deducted. This tends to be more of a problem for intangible assets, because physical assets wear out (therefore, they have ascertainable useful lives). Goodwill is an asset without an ascertainable useful life, so under current law no deduction is allowed for the goodwill purchased in a business acquisition. Thus, the buyer would like to see non-deductible goodwill valued for as low an amount as possible.

The tax law requires goodwill to be valued using the so-called "residual method". Under this method, the value of physical assets and amortizable assets are subtracted from the purchase price, and the remainder is deemed to be the value of the unamortizable goodwill.

> **Example:** Consider the sale of the dental practice discussed above. Assume the parties agreed on a purchase price of $600,000. An appraiser has set the value of the dental equipment at $125,000, and the office equipment at $50,000. The building has been appraised for $200,000. The parties, after lengthy negotiations and computations by their accountants, have determined that the patient list is worth $75,000. The value of these assets is $450,000 ($125,000 + $50,000 + $200,000 + $75,000 = $450,000). Thus, using the residual method, the value of the unamortizable goodwill is $150,000 ($600,000 - $450,000 = $150,000).

Since the value of the physical assets purchased in a business acquisition can be readily determined (e.g., by making reference to recent sales of comparable assets), there is a strong incentive for buyers to identify as many amortizable intangible assets as possible. This is the only practical way to reduce the value of unamortizable goodwill.

This state of affairs has led to a lot of remarkably creative business planning. For example, one buyer placed a value on the "in-place" workforce it was inheriting when it bought a manufacturing facility. The buyer reasoned that, absent the seller's workforce already in place, the buyer would be required to go to considerable expense to retain and train a workforce. Since the buyer's accountants were able to value this "asset" and to assign to it a useful life, the buyer received an amortization deduction for it. The value of this in-place workforce also had the benefit of reducing the value of the buyer's unamortizable goodwill. As you can imagine, efforts such as these have produced a lot of disputes with the IRS. When a taxpayer and the government weren't arguing over whether an intangible asset really existed, they were disputing its useful life (the shorter the life, the greater the annual deductions for the taxpayer).

What's New

OBRA 93 attempts to eliminate the disputes between taxpayers and the government by establishing a uniform set of rules for the amortization of acquired intangible assets, including goodwill. Unfortunately, in doing so, it also creates a whole new set of complexities. As you review this summary of these new rules, try to keep one thing in mind: they only apply to intangible assets your business acquires from another business. If you own an on-going business and develop these assets, these rules do not apply to you.

Generally, OBRA requires all acquired intangible assets to be deducted over a 15-year period. This rule will apply whether the actual useful life is longer or shorter than this period.

This change will have a significant negative impact on at least one type of intangible asset: covenants not to compete. Most covenants not to compete only last for a few years; if they were any longer, a court could declare them unenforceable. Thus, the new rules under OBRA will require buyers to deduct short agreements over long time periods.

Example: A two-year covenant not to compete valued at $60,000 would generate $30,000 deductions in both 19X1 and 19X2. A taxpayer in the 34% corporate bracket would realize a tax savings of $10,200 because of this deduction ($30,000 x 34% = $10,200). Under the new OBRA rules for amortizing intangibles, however, only $4,000 could be deducted for each of the next 15 years for the same covenant ($60,000/15=$4,000). This means that the new rules yield an annual tax savings $8,840 lower than the old rules did ($4,000 x 34% = $1,360; $10,200 - $1,360 = $8,840). Of course, the smaller deduction can be claimed over more years, but this hardly offsets the disadvantage.

OBRA specifically excludes certain types of assets from the 15-year deduction period. First, if you acquire commercial computer software, you can deduct it over three years instead of 15. Commercial computer software includes only those programs you can buy "off the shelf" from a vendor.

A second exception to the 15-year rule arises where a bank acquires the right to service mortgages from another financial institution. (Yes, the right to service mortgages is an intangible asset; this gives you some idea of how clever business advisors had become in this area!) These rights can be written off over a nine year period.

Other intangible assets excluded from the new rules include interests in a certain type of financial instrument known as a "notional principal contract"; stock and partnership interests; interests in land; interests in film, videos, books, and the like, unless purchased as part of a complete business acquisition; patents and copyrights, unless purchased as part of a complete business acquisition; professional sports franchises; and, leasehold interests in existence when OBRA was passed.

This change is generally effective for intangible assets acquired after OBRA was enacted (10 August, 1993). However, this change has been under consideration for quite some time, so OBRA includes a provision which allows businesses to elect to use the new rules for any acquisition made after 25 July, 1991 (the date the change was first proposed). Taxpayers also can elect to apply the old rules to acquisitions made after OBRA's enactment if a binding written contract for the acquisition was in effect before 10 August, 1993.

What to Do

Elect Carefully. While there is no way to avoid the new rules for acquisitions made after OBRA was enacted, a planning opportunity may exist for intangible assets acquired after 25 July, 1991. This change produces winners and losers, depending on the type of intangible asset involved. Covenants not to compete are clear losers, while goodwill is a clear winner (it could never be written off before OBRA). However, you can't pick and choose which assets to apply which rules to, so your business must consider all asset acquisitions since 25 July, 1991 to see if, in the aggregate, it would be better off applying the new rules retroactively.

DEDUCTIONS - TRAVEL EXPENSES OF A SPOUSE

What Was

"Ordinary and necessary" business travel expenses are deductible. If a taxpayer brings a family member (often a spouse) along on business travel, expenses related to the other family member are also deductible business expenses as long as the other family member's presence serves a "bone fide" business purpose. Merely performing some incidental business service would not qualify the family member's travel expenses for a business deduction, but the standard was somewhat liberally applied (by taxpayers if not by IRS).

What's New

Effective 1 January, 1994, OBRA disallows the business deduction for the travel expenses of a family member unless three conditions are met:

(1) the family member must be an employee of the business;

(2) the family member's travel must be for a bona fide business reason; and,

(3) the expenses are "ordinary and necessary".

This prohibition does not apply to deductible moving expenses.

What to Do

Bring Back Airport Gifts. This change is intended to eliminate a perceived abuse, and the prohibition is fairly straight-forward. It is not likely you can plan around it, and you should resign yourself to either not bringing your spouse along or not deducting it. Of course, if your family member meets the three criteria discussed above, you are entitled to the deduction for his or her travel expenses, and should not be squeamish about claiming it.

DEDUCTIONS - BUSINESS MEALS

What Was

Taxpayers are entitled to claim as a business deduction 80% of their ordinary and necessary business meals and entertainment expenses. The expenditures must not be "luxurious", must be for a bona fide business purpose, and the taxpayer must be present at the meal or entertainment in order to claim the deduction. Moreover, in the case of entertainment, a bona fide business discussion must occur either during the meal or immediately before or after it. Additionally, written documentation is required to substantiate deductions in excess of $25.

What's New

Effective 1 January, 1994, OBRA reduces the deductible portion of business meals and entertainment from 80% to 50%. The rationale behind the reduction is that these activities involve a substantial element of personal pleasure, and the 50/50 split more closely approximates the business and personal aspects of business meals and entertainment.

What to Do

Swallow Hard. There really is not any way to plan around this change in the tax law. If you are an employee, you may want to consider discussing with your employer ways you can be made whole for your non-deductible expenditures. This may include grossing up your salary to compensate you for the tax deduction you have lost. Examples of grossing-up are included in the section on Club Dues, below. Keep in mind that, unless you do considerable entertaining, or are a singularly valuable employee, this may not be worth the paperwork from your employer's perspective.

Watch Convention and Seminar Expenses. If you attend a business-related convention or seminar, and meals are included in the registration fee you pay, only 50% of the portion of that registration fee attributable to those meals can be deducted. Most seminar and convention sponsors don't separately state the value of the meals they provide. If you find yourself in this situation, estimate as best you can. As long as you make a good faith attempt to approximate the value of the meals, it should stand up to IRS scrutiny (in fact, they should be impressed by your honesty!).

DEDUCTIONS - CLUB DUES

What Was

Taxpayers are allowed to deduct club dues as a business expense if they use the club more than 50% for business purposes, but can deduct only those expenses directly related to the business use of the club.

> **Example:** Sid paid country club dues of $1,000 in 1992. He uses the club 60% for business -- 40% for directly related business entertainment (e.g., a dinner where a business deal is negotiated), and 20% for "associated" business entertainment (e.g., a cocktail party the evening before a board meeting). Sid's 60% business use met the "more-than-50%-test", so he qualified to deduct his direct expenses. Since Sid's direct expenses were 40%, he could deduct $400 of the $1,000 dues paid on the business schedule of his 1992 return.

The law requires taxpayers who want to claim the deduction to keep records to prove their claims. Membership or initiation fees were never deductible.

What's New

OBRA 93 disallows all deductions for club dues, based on the notion that there is a substantial element of personal pleasure and enjoyment in club activities. Dues paid to business, social, athletic, luncheon, sporting, airline and hotel clubs are among the expenses no longer deductible. These changes take effect on 1 January, 1994.

What to Do

Prepay Expenses. Since the deduction ban doesn't take effect until 1 January, 1994, consider paying in December of 1993 your 1994 club dues. Your club probably bills before the year end, anyway. If it doesn't, contact the club manager and request information on pre-payment options. Don't be greedy, though; the IRS may want to have a chat with you if you try to claim deductions for the next 10 years' dues! Usually, about one year of pre-payments is the most individual taxpayers can claim as deductions on their tax returns, and this rule of thumb probably applies here.

Make Sure You Claim Deductions Still Allowed. Remember, this change only applies to club dues. If you belong to a professional society, union, or other business-related organization, those dues are still deductible, subject to the same rules and limitations you have been using for several years now (i.e., the dues must be ordinary and necessary business expenses). Be sure to claim all of the deductions you are entitled to; your dues to the local bar association, medical society, contractors association, business league, or similar organization remain fully deductible.

Ask Your Employer to "Gross-up" Your Salary. If your club dues are essential to your business activities, you may wish to ask your employer to increase your salary by the amount necessary to reimburse you for the tax deduction you lost. Of course, your employer does not have to agree to do this, and many probably will not. However, it never hurts to ask. The mathematical process by which this is accomplished is called "grossing-up". The formula for grossing up a figure to account for the taxes owed on it is: pre-tax amount/(1 - *r*), where *r* equals your marginal tax rate.

> **Example:** You are in the 28% tax bracket, and pay business-related club dues of $4,000 per year. After 1 January, 1994, these dues are no longer deductible to you, and you have lost a deduction worth $1,120 ($4,000 x 28% = $1,120). If your employer is willing to compensate you for losing this deduction, your salary will have to be increased by $1,555.56 ($1,120/(1 - 0.28) = $1,555.56).

This formula does not consider any Social Security taxes or state and local income taxes you might have to pay, but it does give you "rough justice" in maintaining your current financial position. Besides, if you are negotiating from a position of strength, you can add these rates to your marginal rate and ask your employer to "gross-up" for them, too!

DEDUCTIONS - EXECUTIVE COMPENSATION ABOVE $1 MILLION

What Was

Businesses are entitled to a deduction for the reasonable compensation they pay to their employees. IRS uses a case-by-case approach to determine whether or not compensation is "reasonable". Usually, however, disputes as to the reasonableness of compensation arise only in the context of small or closely-held businesses.

What's New

OBRA 93 imposes a $1 million limit on the deduction publicly-traded corporations may claim for the compensation they pay to some of their executives. The rules describing the limit are fairly complicated, but it's important to remember two things: (1) they only apply to a company's five top-paid executives; and, (2) they only apply to corporations whose stock is publicly-traded. Therefore, this change should affect the compensation packages of only a very few individuals nationwide.

Three categories of compensation are not subject to the $1 million limit: (1) payments to a qualified retirement plan; (2) employer-provided fringe benefits that are excluded from income under the tax law (e.g., health insurance, group term life insurance up to $50,000); and, (3) "qualified performance based compensation". Once compensation to any of the five covered executives exceeds $1 million, unless it takes one of these three forms the excess cannot be deducted by the employer. It is, of course, still includible in income by the employee.

Qualified performance based compensation can take one of three forms:

> (1) commissions paid on income generated directly by the executive (as opposed to, for example, commissions paid on income generated by the entire business unit the executive manages).

(2) compensation based on the attainment of pre-established performance goals. These goals must be established by a compensation committee consisting solely of "outside" directors (i.e., not officers or employees of the company) and must be approved by the shareholders. The compensation committee also must certify in writing that the performance goals have been met.

(3) stock options, as long as they are approved by the corporation's "outside" directors and its shareholders, and can only be exercised at the stock's fair market value.

The change is effective for tax years beginning after 1993. However, written employment contracts entered into before 18 February, 1993 -- the day President Clinton outlined his tax and economic proposals to a joint session of Congress -- are exempt from the new law for as long as those contracts remain in effect.

What to Do

Accelerate Income. If your corporation is affected by the new law, consider accelerating the compensation of its top five executives into the company's 1993 tax year. This will avoid the $1 million cap and give your company one last "unlimited" deduction for the compensation paid to its top executives.

Accentuate Performance. The compensation packages of some of the nation's top executives likely will be re-designed in order to accommodate the new restrictions. Performance-based pay is likely to be accentuated, and structured in such a way as to comply with the new law. If you are one of the individuals whose compensation is affected by this change, you -- and your company -- probably should be thinking along these lines.

DEDUCTIONS - LOBBYING EXPENSES

What Was

Businesses are allowed under the tax law to deduct their "ordinary and necessary" expenses. Lobbying expenses are included among those deductible expenses. Deductible lobbying expenses include those directly related to an appearance or submission before Congress, a state legislature, or a city or county council.

Expenses related to political campaigns and attempts to influence the general public regarding legislative or electoral matters are not deductible business expenses.

What's New

Effective for tax years beginning after 1993, OBRA 93 eliminates virtually all lobbying deductions as an ordinary and necessary business expense. The prohibition extends to Federal lobbying activities with Congress, the President, the Vice President, the White House staff, and Cabinet members, and to state lobbying activities with legislatures and senior executives.

Exceptions exist for in-house lobbying activities, as long as total expenditures do not exceed $2,000. The new restriction does not apply to appearances before any of the covered government entities if the appearance is required by law (e.g., subpoena, civil investigation); these expenses are still deductible. Expenses for lobbying activities on the local (i.e., city or county) level remain deductible.

What to Do

Watch Your Dues Deductions. If you belong to a trade or professional association which maintains a Federal or state government relations department, the part of your annual dues payment attributable to its lobbying activities will no longer be deductible. OBRA 93 requires your association to alert you as to the non-deductible portion of your dues, so be on the look-out for it. (Also consider that it may take some smaller associations time to implement this change.)

DEDUCTIONS - HEALTH INSURANCE COSTS OF SELF-EMPLOYED PERSONS

What Was

When an employer provides health insurance coverage for its employees, the cost of that coverage is a deductible business expense. However, when the employee receiving the coverage is also an owner of the business, that's not always the case. Regular C corporations can deduct the health insurance premiums they pay on behalf of owner-employees, but sole proprietorships, partnerships, and S corporations cannot. Since these last three forms of business are considered "pass-through" entities under the tax law (i.e., items of business income, expense, gain or loss, and credit pass through directly to the owners' personal returns), the health insurance expenses of the owners must be claimed as a personal itemized deduction.

This can work a real hardship for owners of these pass-through entities, which by and large are small businesses. If for some reason the owner does not itemize deductions, the value of the deduction is lost to him or her. Even if the owner does itemize, medical expenses are only allowed as a deduction to the extent they exceed 7.5% of income.

> **Example:** Your income is $40,000. You incur $2,500 of medical expenses in year 19X1. You cannot deduct these expenses on Schedule A, because they are lower than 7.5% of your income ($40,000 x 7.5% = $3,000).

The tax law did allow these business owners to claim 25% of their health insurance premiums as an above-the-line deduction on their individual returns. The remaining 75% could then be claimed as an itemized deduction, if the taxpayer exceeded the 7.5% "floor" on such deductions. However, the provision allowing this limited above-the-line deduction expired 30 June, 1992.

What's New

OBRA 93 reinstated the 25% above-the-line deduction of health insurance premiums for sole proprietors, partners, and S corporation owner-employees. The provision was extended retroactively from 1 July, 1992 through 31 December, 1993.

What to Do

Look for a Refund Opportunity. If you owned one of the three types of businesses affected by this change, and you paid for your health insurance premiums in the second half of 1992, you are entitled to a refund. You should amend your return to claim this deduction for the last six months of 1992.

Stay Tuned. The provision was extended for a relatively short period of time, only until the end of 1993. Congress and the President expect to make this provision permanent (and to expand it from 25% to a full 100%) in the context of health care reform.

DEDUCTIONS - ALTERNATIVE MINIMUM TAX DEPRECIATION

What Was

Property used in a trade or business is depreciated over its useful life. Taxpayers owning such property in essence deduct its purchase price ratably over a number of years. Because an asset's useful life determines how quickly the asset is written off, it also determines how large or small the depreciation deduction for that asset will be each year.

Corporations currently must compute their depreciation deductions three different ways in order to comply with the tax law: once for regular tax purposes, a second time for alternative minimum tax (AMT) purposes, and yet a third time in order to compute something called adjusted current earnings (ACE). This is in addition to any depreciation computations required for accounting purposes.

Generally speaking, AMT depreciation for personal property results in a smaller deduction than regular tax depreciation. This has the effect of raising the amount of income subject to AMT.

ACE is similar in concept to a corporation's earnings and profits. In order to compute ACE, several adjustments to a company's book income must be made. The third depreciation computation, referenced above, is one of those ACE adjustments. It results in an even smaller depreciation allowance for ACE purposes. Once all the ACE adjustments are made, a portion of ACE is added back to income for computing AMT. This ACE depreciation adjustment is separate from the second depreciation adjustment made in computing AMT, discussed above.

What's New

Starting in 1994, corporations no longer have to re-compute depreciation in order to determine their ACE adjustment. They only will have to compute one depreciation adjustment in determining AMT. Thus, there is still an ACE adjustment made in computing AMT, but it won't have a separate depreciation component. This change only applies to property placed in service (i.e., used for the first time) after 1993.

What to Do

Lose That Third Set of Books. This pro-taxpayer change will help simplify record-keeping for most of the nation's corporations. It is expected to be particularly beneficial to capital-intensive enterprises (i.e., businesses that invest heavily in equipment), removing some from the rolls of AMT taxpayers altogether.

CANCELLATION OF INDEBTEDNESS - EXCHANGES OF STOCK FOR DEBT

What Was

Under the tax law, when a taxpayer has outstanding debt forgiven, the amount cancelled is considered to be income to the taxpayer. Generally, the taxpayer must include in income the amount of debt forgiven, and therefore pay tax on it.

> **Example 1:** You have a $5,000 balance on your credit card. You lose your job and can no longer afford to make monthly payments on your debt. You contact the credit card company, and, after explaining your circumstances, you offer to send them $2,500 if they will write off the balance of the loan. The credit card company agrees to your proposal. You have $2,500 in income from the forgiven debt ($5,000 - $2,500 = $2,500).
>
> **Example 2:** You own a house worth $100,000 in a steadily declining real estate market. Your mortgage balance on the house is $110,000. You can no longer afford to pay the mortgage, and convince the bank holding the loan to accept title to the house in exchange for releasing you from your loan obligations. In agreeing to do so, the bank has forgiven $10,000 of your indebtedness ($110,000 - $100,000 = $10,000). It is possible that the $10,000 will be taxable income to you.

Whether or not you have to recognize income on forgiven debt that is secured by property you own (e.g., a car or a house) depends on how much you originally paid for that property, including improvements. It also depends on whether or not you have filed for Federal bankruptcy protection. If you are in bankruptcy, any debts you have forgiven through the bankruptcy process do not generate taxable income for you.

If you qualify for this special bankruptcy treatment, you don't get off scott free, however. The law requires you to reduce certain "tax attributes" by the amount of debt forgiven. Tax attributes are complicated to explain, but they include such things as net operating losses (if you are a business), your "basis" in assets (used to determine your gain or loss when you dispose of those assets), and capital loss carry-forwards (individuals can only deduct $3,000 in excess losses per year; any extra has to be used in subsequent years). Thus, forgiveness of debt in bankruptcy may not generate immediate taxable income, but it can impact your tax returns in future years.

> **Example:** In 19X1, you sold some stock at a $23,000 loss. Since you had no other gains or losses that year, you claimed a $3,000 capital loss on your 19X1 return (the maximum excess capital loss you are allowed to claim in any one year), and carried the remaining $20,000 forward to be used in future years ($23,000 - $3,000 = $20,000) You declare bankruptcy in 19X2. As part of the bankruptcy plan, you have $5,000 in unsecured credit card debts cancelled. Your capital loss carry forward is reduced to $15,000 as a result of the forgiven debt ($20,000 - $5,000 = $15,000).

Sometimes, when a corporation is undergoing a bankruptcy reorganization, it will convince its creditors to accept shares of its stock in exchange for cancelling some or all of the outstanding debt. In these cases, there is no cancellation of indebtedness income, because the corporation has exchanged something of value (its stock) for the debt forgiven.

What's New

Effective for stock transferred after 1994, the so-called "stock-for-debt" exception described above will be repealed. Therefore corporations in bankruptcy who negotiate such exchanges will be required to reduce their tax attributes to the extent of debt forgiven in exchange for stock issued.

A special transition rule indicates that the change will not apply to bankruptcy cases filed before 1 December, 1993.

What to Do

Act Now. If you think your corporation may be negatively impacted by this change, and you are contemplating bankruptcy, consult with an expert now. It may be to your advantage to get your case filed before the 1 December, 1993 deadline for the transition rule.

If you are unable to use the transition rule and are affected by this change, keep in mind that issuing stock to your creditors in exchange for debt forgiveness in Title 11 Bankruptcies will be slightly less attractive now. It may still be your company's only way to work out a reorganization plan, but it will not be as attractive. This change was included because Congress believed that bankrupt corporations were being given an unfair tax advantage as compared to start-up ventures or companies that tried to restructure their debt without going into bankruptcy.

CANCELLATION OF INDEBTEDNESS - PASSIVE LOSSES AND AMT CREDITS

What Was

Under the tax law, when creditor cancels a debt you owe it, the amount forgiven is considered to be income to you. Generally, you must include in income the amount of debt forgiven, and therefore pay tax on it. If you're in bankruptcy, however, any debts forgiven through the bankruptcy process do not generate taxable income. Instead, the law requires you to reduce certain "tax attributes" by the amount of debt forgiven. Tax attributes include such things as net operating losses (if you are a business), your "basis" in assets (used to determine your gain or loss when you dispose of those assets), and capital loss carry-forwards (individuals can only deduct $3,000 in excess losses per year; any extra has to be used in subsequent years). Tax attributes often can be thought of as tax benefits that you carry forward from previous years. Thus, forgiveness of debt in bankruptcy may not generate immediate taxable income, but it can impact your tax returns in future years.

What's New

For tax years beginning after 1993, OBRA adds two new items to the list of tax attributes that must be reduced when debt is forgiven in a bankruptcy context: AMT credits and suspended passive losses and credits.

The AMT credit allows taxpayers to reduce their current regular tax liability by a portion of the AMT they paid in the prior year. Thus, as a result of this change, the amount of cancelled debt can be used to reduce a taxpayer's minimum tax credit, beginning the year after the bankruptcy proceeding is complete.

Passive losses are discussed in the real estate portion of the investment section in the last Chapter of this book. Generally, if you have passive losses in excess of your passive income, and don't qualify for the special $25,000 real estate exception, you must carry those losses forward to offset passive income in future years. This change requires a taxpayer to reduce any passive loss "carryforwards" by the amount of discharged debt.

What to Do

Stay Solvent. While this change is not necessarily designed to make bankruptcy harder, it's not going to make it easier. The rule requiring taxpayers to reduce their tax attributes as a result of income from debt cancelled in bankruptcy proceedings is intended to ensure that the tax on cancelled debt income is only deferred, not eliminated. Adding AMT credits and suspended passive losses to the list of tax attributes just reinforces that goal.

CREDITS - TARGETED JOBS TAX CREDIT

What Was

Through 30 June, 1992, certain employers were eligible to claim a credit against their taxes for first-year wages paid to members of specified groups. These groups included economically-disadvantaged individuals and those with disabilities. The credit was equal to 40% of the first $6,000 in qualified wages, for a maximum per employee credit of $2,400 ($6,000 x 40% = $2,400).

What's New

OBRA 93 retroactively reinstated the credit from 1 July, 1992 through 31 December, 1994.

What to Do

Watch for a Refund Opportunity. If you are an employer who took advantage of the credit, review your records to see if you had employees who would have qualified for the credit in the second half of 1992. If you do and you have already filed a return covering any part of that time period, you can amend your return to claim a refund for the credit you are entitled to.

TAX-ADVANTAGED INVESTMENTS - EMPOWERMENT ZONES AND ENTERPRISE COMMUNITIES

What Was

The tax law currently provides no special incentives for locating business facilities within economically-disadvantaged urban or rural areas.

What's New

OBRA 93 creates several special business incentives for facilities established in two types of areas: empowerment zones and enterprise communities. The government will designate 9 empowerment zones and 95 enterprise communities -- in both urban and rural areas -- in 1994 and 1995. The special tax breaks will be available to business operations established in these special areas after they are designated.

Empowerment zones will offer three advantages to businesses that locate within them: (1) employer wage credits; (2) increased Section 179 expensing; and, (3) tax-exempt bond financing for qualified properties. Only this last break will be available to businesses locating within the 95 enterprise communities.

In order to qualify for most of these tax benefits, a business must be located within an empowerment zone or enterprise community, and at least 35% of its employees must live within that zone or community. With a few exceptions, almost any type of trade or business can qualify for the special tax breaks. However, being a landlord within a zone or community will only qualify a business for special tax breaks if: (1) the leased property is not residential; and, (2) at least half of the business' rental income comes from tenants who qualify as zone or community businesses

Employer Wage Credits. Employers will be allowed to claim a credit of 20% of the first $15,000 in annual wages paid to employees (full-time and part-time) living and working within empowerment zones This results in a maximum $3,000 credit per employee

($15,000 x 20% = $3,000). The employment must exceed 90 days to qualify for the credit. Unlike the other two tax breaks described below, this wage credit is available whether or not the employer qualifies as an empowerment zone business. This means that the credit can be claimed even if fewer than 35% of the business' employees live within the zone.

Section 179 Expensing. Section 179 allows qualifying small businesses to claim an immediate deduction for the purchase of assets that otherwise would have to be depreciated and deducted over a number of years. The mechanics of this provision are described in the section on expensing small business assets earlier in this Chapter.

The $17,500 Section 179 limit is increased to $37,500 for qualified zone businesses who purchase tangible personal assets after their zone is designated and use those assets "substantially" in a zone business.

Tax-Exempt Bonds. OBRA authorizes states to issue tax-exempt bonds to help business owners finance new facilities to be located in empowerment zones and enterprise communities. These bonds will make it easier (and financially more attractive) for businesses that want to locate in zones or communities to do so.

What to Do

Consider Investment in Economically-Distressed Areas. This change provides some incentives for businesses to locate their facilities in enterprise communities, and some serious incentives to locate in empowerment zones. If your business is planning a new facility, this provision merits consideration, and the empowerment zones merit your business' serious exploration. Remember, both urban and rural areas will be designated under the law, and you will have several locations to choose from

TAX ADVANTAGED INVESTMENTS - INDIAN RESERVATIONS

What Was

The tax law currently provides no special incentives for locating business facilities within an Indian Reservation.

What's New

OBRA 93 creates two special business incentives for facilities established on Indian Reservations, both effective on 1 January, 1994.

First, OBRA creates a special accelerated depreciation schedule for property used in the active conduct of a business within an Indian Reservation. This results in higher and quicker depreciation deductions for eligible property. The accelerated depreciation periods are as follows:

Regular Period:	Indian:
3-year property	2 years
5-year property	3 years
7-year property	4 years
10-year property	6 years
15-year property	9 years
20-year property	12 years
non-residential real estate	22 years

Second, OBRA creates an employment credit for wages and health insurance costs paid to members of Indian tribes (and their spouses) working on a Reservation and living on or near it. The credit is equal to 20% of the first $20,000 of annual wages and health insurance paid, for a maximum per employee credit of $4,000 ($20,000 x 20% = $4,000). The credit is not available with respect to employees earning above $30,000 per year. An employer cannot claim both a credit and a business deduction for wages or health insurance expenses paid.

$ What to Do

Consider Indian Investment. This change provides some serious incentives for businesses to locate their facilities on Indian Reservations. Note particularly that you could reduce the depreciation write-off period for an office or factory building from 39 to 22 years by locating on an Indian Reservation. If your business is planning a new facility, this provision merits your consideration.

CREDITS - POSSESSIONS TAX CREDIT

What Was

The tax law allows corporations with operations in U.S. possessions to elect a credit under Section 936 of the Internal Revenue Code. The Section 936 credit is frequently used by corporations with operations in Puerto Rico.

If a corporation chooses to claim the credit (instead of deducting expenses for its possession-based operations), it is equal to the Federal income tax the corporation would pay on: (1) income from the active conduct of a trade or business within the possession; (2) gain from the sale of a business in a possession; and, (3) qualified investment income from the possession.

What's New

For tax years beginning after 1994, OBRA 93 limits the possessions tax credit to one of two limitations: (1) the economic activity limitation; or, (2) the percentage limitation. Unless the corporation elects to use the percentage limitation, the economic activity limitation will apply.

The economic activity limitation will be equal to the sum of: (1) 60% of qualified compensation paid in the possession; (2) a percentage of deductions claimed for depreciation of tangible property used in the possession; and, (3) a portion of the income tax paid to the possession's government.

The percentage limitation is based on the old Section 936 credit. It is equal to 60% of the old credit in 1994, 55% in 1995, 50% in 1996, 45% in 1997, and 40% from 1998 on.

What to Do

Review Plant Site Selections. If your corporation has Puerto Rico-based operations, this change makes them less attractive. You should review your out-year financial projections to see if the scaled-back credit is going to have an inordinate impact on profits. If so, it may be worth evaluating the pros and cons of re-locating. However, the expenses of moving must be considered when evaluating the impact of the new Section 936 credit. Likely, many companies will still find it profitable to do business in Puerto Rico, just less so than it used to be.

CREDITS - RESEARCH & EXPERIMENTATION

What Was

Taxpayers carrying on a trade or business were allowed a 20% credit for their "qualified" research and experimentation expenses, and for grants paid to universities for such research. Qualified expenditures were those additional expenditures above a taxpayer's "base amount". Arriving at one's base amount required a complex set of calculations relating to the business' previous research expenditures and prior gross receipts. Certain "start-up" operations also qualified for the credit.

What's New

OBRA 93 retroactively extends the "R&D" tax credit from 1 July 1992 through 30 June, 1995. It also makes some technical changes to how start-up companies compute their base amounts.

What to Do

Watch for a Refund Opportunity. If your firm took advantage of the credit, review your records to see if you had qualifying R&D expenditures during the second half of 1992. If you do and you have already filed a return covering any part of that time period, you can amend your return to claim a refund for the credit you are entitled to.

ESTIMATED TAXES - COMPUTATION

What Was

Corporations are required to pay their estimated income taxes in quarterly installments. In order to avoid penalties for underpayment of estimated taxes, corporations rely on a safe harbor computation. If the amounts paid-in satisfy the safe harbor computation, no penalty can be assessed for underpayment of tax.

The law provides for two different safe harbors depending on the size of the corporation. "Small" corporations -- those with taxable income that has not exceeded $1 million in any of their three preceding tax years -- can make their estimated payments based on 100% of their prior year's liability. The small corporation's prior tax year must have been a full 12-month year, and the corporation must have had a tax liability in that prior year in order to qualify for this option.

"Large" corporations -- those with taxable income that has exceeded $1 million in any of the three prior tax years, as well as small corporations that fail to qualify for the "100%-of-prior year" method described above, must make estimated payments based on 97% of the current year's tax liability. Note, however, that large corporations can use the "100%-of-prior-year" method available to small corporations to compute their first quarterly installment only. Since it's not always easy to project what your tax liability is going to be for an entire year, this safe harbor isn't really that safe, even for truly large corporations.

What's New

Effective for tax years beginning in 1994, OBRA 93 requires "large" corporations to make their estimated tax payments based on 100% of their current year's tax liability These corporations still will be permitted to use the "100%-of-prior-year" safe harbor for their first required estimated payment

What to Do

Sharpen Your Pencil. If your corporation is affected by these changes, there is no way to avoid them. Your company will have to compute its estimated taxes using the new rules, and it may not be easy!

CHAPTER 5

CHANGES AFFECTING TRUSTS AND DECEDENTS' ESTATES

RATES - ESTATE AND GIFT TAX RATES

What Was

The tax law imposes a tax on certain transfers of property, whether by lifetime gift or inheritance, through a single rate structure. The unified estate and gift tax is levied at 16 separate rates between its 18% minimum and its 50% maximum. The highest rate is imposed on transfers valued above $2,500,000.

Through 31 December, 1992, there had been two higher estate and gift tax brackets. They were 53% and 55%, imposed on transfers above $2.5 million and $3 million, respectively. These rates had expired at the end of 1992.

The estate and gift tax regime is fairly comprehensive. In general, tax is imposed on gifts in excess of $10,000 per year and decedent's estates worth more than $600,000. A sophisticated specialty of tax practice has evolved devoted exclusively to helping taxpayers prepare for and avoid estate and gift taxes.

What's New -

OBRA 93 retroactively revived the two highest estate and gift tax rates -- 53% and 55% -- which had expired last December 31st. The new rates apply to the estates of those dying anytime in 1993, as well as to gifts made anytime in 1993. This means that a few estates for which returns have already been filed may owe more tax. IRS announced earlier this year that it would contact the representatives of any estates affected by this retroactive change.

What to Do

Plan Ahead. While these new rates will affect only a few taxpayers, they emphasize for all the need for proper estate planning. Review the section on estate planning in the last Chapter of this book. After reading it, if you think you have estate tax problems, make an appointment with a qualified estate planner -- pronto!!

RATES - TRUST & ESTATE INCOME TAX RATES

What Was

As of 1 January, 1993, the tax rates imposed on the taxable income of trusts and estates were:

If taxable income is:	The tax is:
Not over $3,750	15% of taxable income
Over $3,750 but not over $11,250	$562.50 plus 28% of the amount over $3,750
Over $11,250	$2,662.50 plus 31% of the amount over $11,250

These rates are indexed for inflation each year. The maximum rate of income taxation on the net capital gains of trusts and estates is 28%.

What's New

OBRA 93 revises the tax rate structure applied to the taxable income of trusts & estates. In addition to adding a 36% bracket and a 10% surtax, OBRA also lowered the thresholds at which the old rates apply. What's more, these changes were made retroactively to 1 January, 1993. This means income a trust or a decedent's estate already has earned may be taxed at higher rates.

The new trust & estate tax rate table for 1993 is:

If taxable income is:	The tax is:
Not over $1.500	15% of taxable income
Over $1,500 but not over $3.500	$225 plus 28% of the amount over $1,500

Over $3,500 but not over $5,500	$785 plus 31% of the amount over $3,500
Over $5,500 but not over $7,500	$1,405 plus 36% of the amount over $5,500
Over $7,500	$2,125 plus 36.9% of the amount over $7,500

These rates will continue to be indexed for inflation, but indexation of the 36% and 39.6% brackets will not occur until 1995.

The installment payment plan available to individual taxpayers hit by retroactive income tax increases (described in the section on individual rate increases in the Chapter on changes affecting individuals) is not available to trusts and decedents' estates affected by this change.

What to Do

Distribute Income. This change represents a serious "hit" for trusts and estates. Higher trust and estate rates kick in at much lower income levels than higher individual tax rates. Fiduciaries now have a stronger incentive than ever to distribute income out to beneficiaries so it can be taxed at their (comparatively) lower rates. If you are a fiduciary, make trust or estate distributions as soon as possible. Practical or legal impediments may make this strategy difficult for some trusts and estates, however, making tax-advantaged investing even more desirable.

Look for Tax-Advantaged Investments. Tax-advantaged investments have been made even more attractive by the new OBRA rates. Tax-exempt municipal bonds are likely to be favored by many investors who fall within the new 36% and 39.6% tax brackets. If you are a trust fiduciary or the personal representative of a decedent's estate, you may want to consider this option. Review the section on tax-advantaged investing in the last Chapter of this book to learn how to maximize your investment dollars. Keep in mind, however, that state law or your governing instrument may limit your range of investment choices. Always remember that your fiduciary obligations must take priority over considerations such as after-tax rate of return.

Seek Capital Gains. If you are the fiduciary of a trust or estate affected by the new top brackets, you now have a greater incentive to seek investment vehicles which emphasize capital gains (as opposed to interest or dividends). The top income tax rate is 39.6%, but OBRA left the top rate on capital gains at 28%. This differential makes investments that declare capital gains (such as some growth mutual funds) more attractive to taxpayers in the new brackets. Again, however, before acting, make sure your proposed investments are legal and consistent with your fiduciary obligations.

Watch Your Estimated Tax Payments. Remember that OBRA's higher rates -- and lower brackets -- went into effect last January 1st. If your trust or estate's going to be in these new higher brackets, you have an estimated tax payment problem. At least two (and probably three) of your quarterly estimated payments were not based on the new rates. You're going to owe money next April 15th (assuming your trust or estate is on a calendar year).

If you are the fiduciary of a trust or decedent's estate, you may want to adjust for this problem now. Make higher estimated tax payments for the rest of the year, in order to make sure that you won't have to write a big check when the next return is due. Even better, start putting the money aside now so you can pay it at tax time without cramping your trust or estate's cash flow. This way, you earn interest on the money, not the government. OBRA 93 contains language indicating that you can't be penalized for under-payment of estimated taxes in 1993, as long as the under-payment is only attributable to the rate hikes. Regardless of your method, you should be planning ahead for next year's unpleasantness.

CHAPTER 6

CHANGES AFFECTING REAL ESTATE

PASSIVE LOSSES - RULES FOR REAL ESTATE PROFESSIONALS

What Was

The tax law generally allows you to claim losses for passive activities only to offset your income from those activities. In other words, you generally cannot use excess passive losses to reduce your other sources of income.

Passive activities are those in which you do not "materially participate"; investments in limited partnerships are a typical example of passive activities. This restriction was added to the law because high income taxpayers in the late 70's and early 80's were making investments based on their tax deductions, not their income potential. These so-called tax shelters were used to reduce the amount of income from other sources on which tax had to be paid. The investments rarely generated any money for their investors, just tax deductions.

The tax law defines all real estate investments as passive activities. This would mean that excess real estate losses could not be used to offset other income. However, there is a limited exception to this rule for certain real estate activities which generate losses under $25,000 per year. Thus, real estate losses can produce only a limited offset against other income. Still, this rule provides an important tax shelter. It is discussed in the real estate portion of the investments section in the last Chapter of this book.

The inclusion of real estate activities in the definition of passive activities has created a hardship for taxpayers who work in the real estate business. Although their real estate activities constitute their trade or business, their ability to deduct legitimate business losses is limited by the passive activity rules.

> **Example:** You are a real estate professional. You own and manage many rental properties. Because of the bad economy this year, these properties generated $30,000 in losses. You also earn $40,000 in interest income this year. Even

if you "actively participate" in the management of these properties (and you do), only $25,000 of these losses can be used to offset your interest income, due to the limits imposed by the passive activity rules. The remaining $5,000 ($30,000 - $25,000 = $5,000) must be carried forward for possible deduction in a future year. You have net income of $15,000 ($40,000 - $25,000 = $15,000).

Note that, in this example, if you were in any other line of business, your business losses could be used fully to offset your other income.

What's New

OBRA 93 provides relief from the limits of the passive activity rules for certain real estate professionals. In order to qualify for the relief, a taxpayer must spend more than 50% of his or her time in the real estate business. The minimum time spent in any year must exceed 750 hours. Employees of real estate businesses only qualify for this relief if they are more than 5% owners of the business.

Once you qualify as a real estate professional, you may use your rental real estate losses to offset your other income without regard to the $25,000 limit. However, you still will be subject to the overall limits on deducting passive losses in excess of your passive income.

Example: In the example above, you will be able to use your full $30,000 in passive losses to offset your interest income, leaving you with $10,000 in net income ($40,000 - $30,000 = $10,000).

This change applies to tax years beginning in 1994.

What to Do

Get Active! If you are a real estate professional, make sure you qualify for the special relief created by this change. Once you do, take full advantage of this pro-taxpayer change.

EXCLUSIONS FROM INCOME - DISCHARGED REAL ESTATE DEBT

What Was

When a creditor discharges all or part of a debt, the amount discharged generally is taxable income to the debtor. Certain bankruptcy transactions are an exception to this rule.

What's New

OBRA 93 creates a new exception to the rule requiring discharged debt to be included in income. The exception applies to restructured business real estate debt, but not if the business is a C corporation. All other business entities qualify for the exception.

The exception allows you to exclude from income discharged real estate debt up to two limits: (1) the amount you exclude can't exceed the property's fair market value, minus any other debt secured by it; and, (2) the amount you exclude can't exceed your adjusted basis in the property. Your adjusted basis usually equals the amount you paid for the property plus any capital improvements you've made to it, minus any depreciation you've claimed for it.

> **Example:** You own a building used in your business. On 1 July, 1993, the building is worth $150,000, and is subject to a first mortgage of $110,000 and a second mortgage of $90,000. The bank holding the note on the second mortgage agrees to reduce it to $30,000. Normally, this would result in $60,000 discharge of indebtedness income ($90,000 - $30,000 = $60,000). However, assuming your adjusted basis is greater than $50,000, you could elect to exclude from income $50,000 of the $60,000 debt forgiven. That's because $50,000 is the amount by which the debt being discharged ($90,000) exceeds the fair market value of the property ($150,000), minus any other debt ($110,000) secured by it (i.e., [$90,000 - ($150,000 - $110,000)] = ($90,000 - $40,000) = $50,000). The remaining $10,000 in forgiven debt would still be included in income under the new rule ($60,000 - $50,000 = $10,000)

The change is effective for discharges after 1992.

$ What to Do

Exclude Qualifying Debt Forgiveness from Income. If you own business property secured by debt which is reduced or forgiven by your creditor, take maximum advantage of this pro-taxpayer change. OBRA included this provision to assist business taxpayers faced with declining real estate values in trying to "work-out" (i.e., restructure) their mortgage debts.

DEPRECIATION - NON-RESIDENTIAL REAL PROPERTY

What Was

When you used non-residential real property either in a trade or business or as an investment, the tax law determined the useful life for that property to be 31.5 years. Thus, depreciation deductions for the cost of the property were spread out over that period of time.

What's New

OBRA 93 changed the useful life for non-residential real property from 31.5 years to 39 years. The change generally is effective for property placed in service after 12 May, 1993. However, if construction began before that date or there was a binding contract for the purchase of property before that date, the 31.5 year useful life will apply, as long as the property is placed in service before the end of 1993.

What to Do

Close the Deal. If you entered into a contract for non-residential realty or began constructing such property before 12 May, 1993, you have a strong incentive to try and occupy the property before December 31st. If you can do so, you will fall under the old -- shorter -- useful life, which means you will qualify for bigger depreciation deductions. Light a fire under your builder or seller!

CREDITS - LOW INCOME HOUSING CREDIT

What Was

Until 30 June, 1992, the tax law provided a credit for certain investments in newly constructed or substantially rehabilitated low-income rental housing. Computing the credit involved some intricate math, but it normally was equal to 70% of the cost of the housing, and was claimed in equal annual installments over 10 years. Building owners generally were required to get authority for the credits from a state government agency.

What's New

OBRA 93 made the credit permanent retroactively to 1 July, 1992. It also made some minor technical changes to the way the credit works.

What to Do

Investigate Low Income Housing. The low income housing credit can create an attractive tax advantage for investors in the new higher brackets. If you are affected by the individual rate increases, and have a portfolio large and diversified enough to include real estate investments, property eligible for the credit is worth investigating. Consult your financial advisor for qualifying projects in your area.

TAX-ADVANTAGED INVESTMENTS - QUALIFIED MORTGAGE BONDS & CREDIT CERTIFICATES

What Was

The tax law authorized state and local governments to issue qualified mortgage bonds. These bonds are used to finance the purchase or rehabilitation of single-family, owner-occupied residences. The authority to issue these bonds expired 30 June, 1992.

The tax law also authorized states and localities to use their bond authority to issue mortgage credit certificates instead. These certificates entitled taxpayers who owned homes which would qualify for the revenue bonds to claim a non-refundable credit on their tax returns for a portion of the mortgage interest they paid. The authority to issue these credit certificates also expired 30 June, 1992.

What's New

OBRA 93 makes permanent the authority to issue qualified mortgage bonds and mortgage credit certificates.

What to Do

Check It Out. If you are a moderate-income taxpayer interested in purchasing a house, contact your state or local housing agency to see how the bonds and/or credits work in your area and whether or not you qualify. If you do, take advantage of this pro-taxpayer change.

CHAPTER 7

CHANGES AFFECTING INVESTORS

ABUSIVE TRANSACTIONS - CONVERTING ORDINARY INCOME TO CAPITAL GAINS

What Was

When the tax law imposes different rates of taxation on capital gains and other sources of income ("ordinary income"), an incentive is created for investors to engage in sophisticated techniques to "convert" their ordinary income into capital gains. Doing so enables them to enjoy the benefit of lower capital gains rates.

The tax law contains some provisions to combat these schemes, but recently there has not been much difference between the top regular tax rate and the top capital gains rate. So, nobody really engaged in any fancy transactions that would put the strength of these rules to the test.

What's New

OBRA 93 creates a large differential between the top rate of tax imposed on capital gains and the top rate imposed on ordinary income -- 28% versus 39.6%. This raises the possibility that taxpayers will attempt to maneuver their income from the "ordinary" column to the "capital gains" column. OBRA therefore contains five provisions which are designed to impede such efforts.

Capital Gains Excluded from Investment Income. Taxpayers who itemize can claim a deduction for their investment interest expenses. These expenses are only deductible, however, to the extent of net investment income.

> **Example:** In 19X1 you have $5,000 in net investment income from dividends and capital gains/losses, and $5,100 in investment interest expenses. You report your capital gains and losses on Schedule D, your dividend income on Schedule B, and your investment interest expenses on Schedule A. However, only $5,000 of your $5,100 investment interest expenses can be deducted in the current year, since that is the extent of your net investment income.

Effective 1 January, 1993, net capital gains will no longer be taken into account when computing your net investment income for purposes of claiming a Schedule A investment interest expense deduction. This change will have the effect of lowering your investment expense deduction if your portfolio's return is laden with capital gains.

Definition of Substantially Appreciated Inventory Expanded. When partnerships make distributions of inventory to their partners, these distributions generate ordinary income for the partner if the inventory has "substantially appreciated". For sales and exchanges after 30 April, 1993, OBRA broadens the definition of inventory that is deemed to be "substantially appreciated" under the tax law. Generally, if a partnership's inventory is worth more than 120% of what the partnership paid for it, it will be considered substantially appreciated and taxed as ordinary income when distributed to a partner.

Exceptions to Market Discount Rules Repealed. If an investor sells certain discounted bonds at a profit, the amount of the proceeds attributable to the discount are deemed ordinary income; the remainder generates a capital gain. Exception: this rule doesn't apply to bonds issued before 19 July 1984, or to tax-exempt bonds. OBRA 93 repeals this exception for purchases after 30 April, 1993.

> **Suggestion:** If you purchased bonds before 1 May, 1993 that qualified for the old exception, OBRA may have given you an incentive to hang onto them. Consult with your financial advisor.

Stripped Preferred Stock Subject to OID Rules. The tax law requires an investor holding an original issue discount (OID) bond to include a certain portion of the OID in income each year. OBRA requires appreciation on stripped preferred stock (preferred stock stripped of its dividend rights) to be treated in the same way OID is treated. Thus, the "OID" of stripped preferred stock will be treated as ordinary income. The change is effective for stripped stock purchased after 30 April, 1993.

Transactions Equivalent to Loans Generate Ordinary Income. OBRA 93 requires taxpayers to treat as ordinary income the capital gains generated by transactions that are fundamentally equivalent to loans. OBRA refers to these deals as "conversion transactions". Conversion transactions can occur where an investor holds two positions with respect to the same property, and the investor's net return is attributable to the time value of the funds invested. This puts the investor in the same economic position as a lender, and the interest lenders earn is ordinary income, not capital gains.

The following transactions are specifically treated as conversion transactions: (1) transactions where property is acquired and there is a contemporaneous agreement to sell the same property in the future; (2) straddle transactions; (3) transactions marketed to investors on the basis that they would function like loans but return capital gains instead of ordinary income; and, (4) transactions described as a conversion transaction in regulations to be issued by IRS.

The portion of such transactions to be treated as ordinary income is computed based on the amount of interest that would have accrued to the investor using 120% of the applicable Federal rate (an interest rate published periodically by IRS).

> **Example:** You purchase stock for $100 on 1 January 19X1, and on the same day agree to sell it to Joe's Brokerage on 1 January 19X3 for $115. Assume the applicable Federal rate is 5%. On 1 January, 19X3, you deliver the stock to Joe's and receive $115. Under prior law, you would have recognized $15 in capital gain from the sale of your stock ($115 - $100 = $15). Under this new OBRA provision, $12.36 of that amount would be recharacterized as ordinary income (120% x 5% = 6%; 6% compounded for 2 years x $100 = $12.36).

What to Do

Steer Clear of the Restrictions. If you are caught up in one of these five new restrictions, there really is no way to plan around it. Moreover, if you or your advisor manage to find a way to "convert" ordinary income into capital gains without running afoul of these provisions, keep in mind that the IRS still has its old arsenal of enforcement mechanisms and penalties to keep you in line! IRS will get aggressive if it perceives a revitalization of the old "tax shelter" industry. Steer clear of these problems.

CAPITAL GAINS EXCLUSION - SMALL BUSINESS STOCK

What Was

Net long-term capital gains are taxed at an individual investor's regular tax rate, subject to a maximum rate of 28%. The 28% maximum rate applies even if the taxpayer's other income is taxed in a higher bracket. Previous law allowed a portion of long-term capital gains to be excluded from income, but such a provision is not currently a part of the tax law.

What's New

OBRA 93 creates a limited capital gains exclusion for certain investors, effective for stock issued after 10 August, 1993. C corporations are not eligible to claim the exclusion, but all other taxpayers are. If you meet the conditions for the exclusion, you can exclude from income 50% of the gain you realize when you sell qualifying small business stock.

Only certain stock will qualify for the 50% exclusion. In order to qualify, the small business must be a C corporation with gross assets under $50 million. The stock of certain types of C corporations, such as regulated investment companies, personal service corporations (lawyers, accountants, architects, and health care professionals), and real estate investment trusts, are not covered by the exclusion. Also outside the new exclusion are stocks of corporations in the following industries: banking, leasing, real estate, insurance, farming, mineral extraction, hotels, motels, and restaurants.

With regard to the $50 million asset limit, the exclusion is available as long as the limit is observed when the stock is issued. If the corporation's assets later exceed the $50 million limit, the holder of stock issued before then will still qualify for the exclusion. However, the corporation itself may never again issue stock that qualifies for the exclusion.

Additionally, the stock must be acquired as an original issue, either from the corporation or from a broker, or it may not be eligible for this special treatment.

In order to qualify for this break, you must hold the stock for at least five years. This means that, at the very earliest, any stock sold before 10 August, 1998 will not be eligible for the exclusion.

There is one possible downside to this change: half of the amount of gain excluded from income is a preference item for purposes of computing the alternative minimum tax. In effect, then, 75% of the gain on sales of qualified small business stock is included in computing AMT (50% of gain included for regular tax purposes + (50% x 50%) included for AMT purposes = 50% + 25% = 75%).

What to Do

Look for Investments That Qualify. This provision creates a tremendous tax incentive; qualifying capital gains will effectively be taxed at a maximum rate of only 14% (28% x 50% = 14%). Qualifying small business investments can be a real deal after OBRA. Keep in mind, however, that, as always, your investment must first and foremost be a good investment. If you sink your money into a losing proposition, there isn't much of a tax break in excluding 50% of nothing from your income!

CAPITAL GAINS DEFERRAL - ROLLOVER TO SMALL BUSINESS INVESTMENT COMPANIES

What Was

Generally, when a taxpayer sells a capital asset at a gain, he or she must pay tax on the gain, at a maximum rate of 28%. Certain provisions of the tax law allow taxpayers to defer their gain if they reinvest the proceeds in similar assets, but these special provisions do not apply to sales of publicly-traded stocks. Thus, there is effectively no way to defer taxation on gain from sales of publicly-traded stock.

What's New

Effective for sales made after 10 August, 1993, OBRA allows certain taxpayers to defer gain on the sale of publicly-traded stock if the proceeds are reinvested in a "specialized small business investment company (SSBIC)". An SSBIC is an investment partnership or corporation licensed by the U.S. Small Business Administration to invest a mix of private and SBA-guaranteed capital in minority-owned businesses. Predictably, there are several restrictions on your ability to take advantage of this break.

First, in order to take advantage of this change, you must be an individual or C corporation; trusts, estates, partnerships and S corporations are not eligible for the rollover of gain.

Next, you must invest in the SSBIC within 60 days of selling your old stock. If you wait beyond this point, you can't qualify for the deferral.

There also are two limits on the amount of gain you can rollover into the SSBIC investment: an annual limit of $50,000 for individuals and $250,000 for C corporations; and, a lifetime limit of $500,000 for individuals and $1 million for C corporations. Once the annual limit is exceeded, you cannot defer any additional gain that year. (The individual limits are halved for married taxpayers filing separately.) Once the lifetime limit is reached, you are no longer eligible to defer your capital gains by investing in an SSBIC

$ What to Do

Consider an SSBIC Investment. If you are in a position where you've decided to sell highly-appreciated stock, consult with your financial advisor about the SSBIC option. It may be a way to get out of your old investment while postponing the tax you'd otherwise pay. Of course, the SSBIC you invest in should be sound, and such an investment should be consistent with your overall portfolio and risk tolerance.

CHAPTER 8

CHANGES AFFECTING IRS PROCEDURES

TAX PENALTIES - ACCURACY RELATED AND RETURN PREPARER PENALTIES

What Was

The tax law imposes a penalty on taxpayers who "substantially understate" their tax liabilities or who take a position on a tax return that is either negligent or in disregard of IRS regulations. An understatement of one's tax liability is generally deemed "substantial" if it exceeds 10% of the amount due or $5,000, whichever is greater. The $5,000 threshold is higher for some corporations. The penalty is equal to 20% of the amount of underpaid tax attributable to any of the actions outlined above.

There are rules which allow a taxpayer to reduce the amount of his or her substantial understatement, thereby lowering the amount of the penalty. One of those rules provides an exception to the penalty where the taxpayer takes a position on a tax return that is "not frivolous" and discloses that position on the return. "Taking a position" on a return basically refers to the process of deciding whether a dollar amount or other information you enter on a return is proper or not.

What's New

OBRA raises the ante on the exception to the 20% penalty described above. In order to avoid the penalty, a disclosed position on a tax return can't just be "not frivolous"; instead, it must have a "reasonable basis". A "reasonable basis" is intended to impose a higher standard on taxpayers; the congressional committee report accompanying OBRA indicates that the position taken must be more than "arguable" in order to satisfy the new standard.

The change is effective for returns filed after 1993

$ **What to Do**

Be Careful With Aggressive Return Positions. If you are taking an aggressive return position, and that position affects your total liability by more than 10%, in most cases you probably should have some rule, regulation, or case to support the position you've taken. If you don't, at least be absolutely certain that the IRS doesn't have some ruling or case to back up the opposite position. Otherwise, you run the risk of the 20% penalty for substantial understatement. Don't ever be afraid to claim deductions or credits you're entitled to, just know the risks and proceed with caution when you're not certain.

TAX REFUNDS - INTEREST ON REFUNDS

What Was

Generally speaking, when IRS owes a taxpayer money because the taxpayer has claimed a refund on an original tax return, it must pay the refund (or disallow it) within 45 days. Otherwise, the government must begin to pay interest on the money it owes the taxpayer.

For amended returns claiming refunds, IRS generally is required to pay interest up to the date the payment is made, beginning from the date the return is due or the date it is filed, whichever is later.

What's New

Beginning in 1994, IRS has a 45-day interest free grace period in which to process all refund claims.

$ What to Do

Pick Your Filing Time Carefully. This really is a minor change, overall, but it could have an impact on businesses that file large refund claims based on net operating loss carrybacks. If your business is in this situation, you may want to keep in mind when IRS' "busy times" are, and plan your filings accordingly. The interest clock is only suspended for the 45 days IRS has to process your refund request, so the timing can help. The peak periods at IRS service centers usually are:

March & April - corporate and individual returns

August - individual extensions

September - corporate extensions

October - individual final extensions

INFORMATION RETURNS - DISCHARGE OF INDEBTEDNESS

What Was

Usually, when a creditor discharges a debt, the amount discharged is income to the debtor.

The tax law imposes "information reporting" obligations on a wide variety of business entities who pay money to others. Institutions that pay interest and dividends are among the many payors who file with IRS Forms 1099 each year. Employers file Forms W-2. The list is very extensive. It does not currently include, however, creditors who forgive debt.

What's New

OBRA 93 requires certain financial institutions (e.g., banks, credit unions, Federal agencies) to report to IRS the amount of debt they've forgiven and the name, address and taxpayer ID of the person or business whose debt has been forgiven. The requirement applies to amounts over $600. The requirement is effective for debt discharged after 1993.

What to Do

"Paper" Your Return. Obviously, if you are required to include forgiven debt in your income, you should already be doing so. This change should have no effect on you if you are obeying the law. However, if you are not required to report forgiven debt as income, you may have a small problem. Your creditor is not required to determine whether or not your forgiven debt is taxable; it's just supposed to send the required information to IRS. Then, it's between you and the government. You may want to attach an explanation to your return if you are in a situation where an information return is filed on you but you are not required to report forgiven debt in income. This might (possibly) preempt an unwanted contact from IRS.

CHAPTER 9

OTHER IMPORTANT CHANGES

EXCISE TAXES - "LUXURY" EXCISE TAX

What Was

In 1990, Congress passed a 10% excise tax on the sale of certain luxury items -- cars, boats, planes, jewelry, and furs. The tax was levied on the amount of a purchase exceeding specified base amounts: $30,000 for cars, $100,000 for boats, $250,000 for planes, $10,000 for jewelry, and $10,000 for furs. The taxes have become popularly known as "luxury excise taxes".

> **Example 1:** Jane buys a Speedo 2000 sportscar for $35,000. The dealer will collect an excise tax of $500 from her. This tax is computed by subtracting the base amount from the purchase price ($35,000 - $30,000 = $5,000) and multiplying the result by the tax rate ($5,000 x 10% = $500).

> **Example 2:** Jane buys a Speedo 1500 sportscar for $25,000. The dealer will not collect any excise tax from her, since the purchase price ($25,000) is less than the base amount ($30,000).

The tax even applied when affected items were brought in for repairs and alterations and the value of the repaired or altered item exceeded the base amount. This rule proved particularly vexing for people who brought gemstones into jewelers for resettings or for people who sought to have their furs restyled.

What's New

Many critics argued that the tax was hurting US industries, particularly the boating industry; people simply went to the Caribbean to purchase their yachts, thereby avoiding the tax. Additionally, the revenues raised by the taxes never met original expectations. Therefore, OBRA repealed the luxury excise tax with respect to boats, planes, jewels, and furs, effective 1 January, 1993.

The tax was not completely repealed for automobiles, but several important changes were made. First, IRS now will increase the base amount for cars to account for inflation. The adjustments will occur whenever inflation causes the base amount to increase by an increment of $2,000 over its original $30,000. Thus, while the base will remain at $30,000 for the rest of 1993, it will increase to $32,000 in 1994.

Next, the new law specifies that the tax does not apply to any devices or accessories installed on a passenger vehicle to make the vehicle accessible or operable by people with disabilities. The law indicates that this special exception does not apply to common dealer accessories such as power windows, power door locks, power seats, or power windows. This change is effective for purchases made after 1990.

Finally, the new law exempts dealer demonstration vehicles ("demos") from the tax. The exemption applies to vehicles first used in 1993.

What to Do

Be Careful Making New Purchases. Except in the case of automobiles, retailers are no longer required to collect the luxury excise tax. Any dealer of boats, planes, jewels, or furs who tells you that they still must collect the tax is wrong. Such assertions should make you suspicious of other aspects of the deal you may be negotiating with them. You *do not* have to pay this tax anymore. In the case of cars, make sure the tax is only charged on the amount of your purchase exceeding the 1993 base rate of $30,000.

See If You Are Entitled to a Refund. Because the tax was repealed retroactively with respect to everything except autos, you may be eligible to claim a refund for any taxes you paid on purchases made in 1993 (as well as on purchases in 1992 or 1991 for accessories making a car handicapped-accessible). If you bought an expensive boat, plane, jewelry or fur this year, review your receipt to see if you paid any Federal excise tax (remember that state and local taxes are not affected by this change). If you paid this tax you may be eligible to claim a refund.

What if you can't tell whether or not you paid any tax? If the purchase price was over the base amounts (indicated above), the dealer was required to collect the tax, so it probably was built into your sales price (even if the dealer failed to separately state it on your invoice). If you're at all unsure, check with your dealer; they can tell you whether you paid the tax.

The dealer is also the place to go to claim a refund of any tax paid. The law requires dealers to refund the taxes paid by consumers and then to claim a refund or credit from the government in order to make themselves whole.

EXCISE TAXES - TRANSPORTATION FUELS TAX

What Was

The tax law imposes a variety of excise taxes on transportation fuels. Before OBRA, gasoline and other fuels used by highway vehicles and motorboats was taxed at 14.1 cents per gallon, diesel fuel at 20.1 cents per gallon, non-commercial aviation gasoline at 15.1 cents per gallon, non-commercial aviation jet fuel at 17.6 cents per gallon, commercial aviation fuel at 0.1 cents per gallon, railroad diesel fuel at 2.6 cents per gallon, and inland waterways fuels at 17.1 cents per gallon (increases in 1994 and 1995 will put the tax on this last fuel at 20.1 cents per gallon).

What's New

Effective 1 October, 1993, OBRA 93 increased the excise tax on virtually all transportation fuels by 4.3 cents per gallon. It also for the first time imposed the tax on liquified natural gas and compressed natural gas used in highway vehicles or motorboats. Important exemptions from this increase include home heating oil (diesel #2) and gasoline and diesel fuels used on farms.

The new law also extends the existing diesel fuel excise tax to noncommercial motorboat uses, effective 1 January, 1994.

What to Do

Conserve! There is no way to avoid an excise tax increase except to buy less of what is being taxed. In the case of transportation fuels, this means consumers should become more conscious of the mileage their vehicles are attaining. Proper maintenance can help keep mileage levels high. Of course, the modest rate of increase -- 4.3 cents per gallon -- doesn't offer much incentive by itself, but the total Federal and state tax on transportation fuels is beginning to add up. Also, there's no reason to believe future increases won't happen, since the United States has the cheapest gasoline in the industrialized world. The actions you take now to minimize the impact of transportation excise taxes ultimately will pay off for you, your pocketbook, and the environment!

CREDITS - CONTRIBUTIONS TO COMMUNITY DEVELOPMENT CORPORATIONS

What Was

Taxpayers are allowed to claim deductions for their contributions to qualified charities, up to specified limits. The deductions for individuals usually are limited to 50% of income, although these limits can be lower depending on the type of property contributed and the type of organization it is contributed to. The annual limit for corporations is 10% of income. Contributions in excess of these limits can be carried forward and applied to future years, for up to five years.

What's New

OBRA 93 creates a special kind of contribution which is eligible for a tax credit instead of a deduction. The credit is available for certain contributions to a "community development corporation (CDC)". OBRA empowers the Secretary of the U.S. Department of Housing and Urban Development to designate up to 20 CDCs nationwide. The CDCs will provide employment and business opportunities to low-income individuals within their operating areas. Each CDC will be limited to accepting a maximum of $2 million in contributions.

The credit is limited to 5% of the amount contributed, spread out over 10 years. Thus, after 10 years have passed, the total credit claimed will equal 50% of the amount contributed (10 x 5% = 50%). Additionally, contributions must be in cash, and not in property.

In order to qualify, the cash contribution must be available to the CDC for at least 10 years. Thus, the credit is available for a loan to a CDC that is at least 10 years long, even if the principal must be returned to the contributor after that period.

For outright contributions to CDCs (as opposed to loans), the credit claimed is in addition to any charitable contribution the taxpayer could claim for his or her donation.

The provision is effective 10 August, 1993.

$ What to Do

Look Into CDCs. At this point, it's not clear how widely-available CDC contribution credits will be; with only 20 CDCs authorized under OBRA, and only $2 million in contributions permitted per CDC, the $40 million in available credits may well be quickly snapped up. If you are able to latch onto one, however, they represent a tax-smart way to make contributions in needy areas. They should be particularly attractive to businesses with planned giving programs.

CHECK-OFFS - PRESIDENTIAL ELECTION CAMPAIGN FUND

What Was

The Federal election laws provide for the public financing of presidential campaigns. Candidates running for president who accept Federal funds agree not to accept private contributions for their campaigns. The theory behind the law is that public financing of presidential elections will result in less influence being exerted by so-called "special interests".

The amount of Federal money provided for presidential campaigns is determined by individual American taxpayers through a "check-off" included on their Federal tax returns. Taxpayers are asked to check "yes" if they wish to "contribute" $1 to the Presidential Election Campaign Fund, and "no" if they do not. Although checking "yes" does increase the contributions to the fund by $1, the check-off does not affect a taxpayer's bill. That is, if a taxpayer checks the "yes" box, his or her tax liability does not go up by $1. Similarly, a taxpayer checking the "no" box does not realize a $1 reduction in his or her tax liability.

What's New

OBRA 93 increases the amount of each check-off "contribution" to the Presidential Election Campaign Fund from $1 to $3, starting in 1994.

$ What to Do

Make an Informed Choice. Some people check "no" when asked about the Presidential Election Campaign Fund for the wrong reason. They think that checking "yes" is giving those "crooks in Washington" more of the taxpayers' hard-earned money. This may or may not be true, but the question being asked by the check-off is whether the money for presidential campaigns should come from individual citizens or "special interests". If you believe that public financing of presidential campaigns is preferable to private contributions, you should check "yes" on your tax return, regardless of your distaste for particular politicians. Of course, if for philosophical reasons you are opposed to public financing of campaigns, "no" is the box you should be checking. In either case, it is important to be sure that you make an informed choice; you should understand what the check-off is really for before deciding what to do.

CHAPTER 10

BASIC TAX PLANNING OPPORTUNITIES

TAX SAVINGS WHEN SELLING YOUR HOME

When you sell the house you live in, the tax law generally requires you to pay tax on any gain you recognize. The gain is computed by subtracting the amount you paid for the property from its sales price; you can use the cost of any improvements you made to the home (but not repairs) and most of the expenses of selling your home (broker's commissions, transfer taxes you pay, etc.) to reduce the gain.

> **Example 1:** You purchased your home 10 years ago for $100,000. You sell it today for $150,000, paying $10,000 in broker's commissions, transfer taxes, and settlement charges. Your gain is $40,000 ($150,000 - $10,000 - $100,000 = $40,000).

> **Example 2:** Same facts as above, except you also put a $15,000 addition on your house a few years ago. Now, your gain is $25,000 ($150,000 - $10,000 - $100,000 - $15,000 = $25,000).

If you've lived in your house for a number of years, inflation alone will probably leave you with a substantial gain when you sell. There are two important tax breaks you can use, however, to postpone or even eliminate some of this gain.

Deferring Gain

Under certain circumstances, you can defer the gain you recognize when selling your old home by "rolling it over" into a new one. Here's the catch: you must pay at least as much for the new home as you received for the old one. When you roll over the gain into a new home, you postpone paying the tax on it until you sell your new home. Be aware, however, this special provision does have one funny wrinkle to it. If you qualify to roll over your gain, it is mandatory that you do so.

> **Example 1:** You sell your primary residence for $140,000 and immediately buy a new one for $145,000. Any gain

you may have on the sale of the old residence can be "rolled over" into the new home.

Example 2: You sell your primary residence for $140,000, and pay a broker's commission of $5,000. You immediately buy a new home for $138,000 dollars. You still qualify to "roll over" your gain because your "adjusted sales price" ($140,000 - $5,000 = $135,000) is lower than your purchase price ($138,000).

There is one other important restriction on your ability to use this tax-deferral technique: settlement on the sale of your old home and on the purchase of your new home must occur within two years of each other. The law gives you additional time if you are in the military or move overseas.

A final tip to help lower your gain: normally, "fix-up expenses" -- minor landscaping, painting, wallpapering, etc. -- are not deductible when spent on your primary residence. However, if you incur these fix-up expenses within 90 days of entering into a sales contract, you can use them to lower any gain you qualify to postpone.

Example 1: You paid $100,000 for your primary residence 10 years ago. You sell it for $140,000, and pay a broker's commission of $5,000. 30 days before the sales contract is signed, you pay $4,000 to have the exterior of your home painted. You immediately purchase a new residence worth $140,000. You qualify to roll over a gain of $31,000 ($140,000 - $5,000 - $100,000 - $4,000 = $31,000).

If you are unable to take advantage of the deferral rules, fix-up expenses cannot be used to lower the amount of your gain.

Example 2: Same facts as above, except you do not buy a replacement residence. Your gain is $35,000 ($140,000 - $5,000 - $100,000 = $35,000). No reduction is made for your fix-up expenses.

Similarly, fix-up expenses may be used to lower your gain, but not to help you qualify for roll over treatment.

> **Example 3:** Same facts as in Example 1, except your new residence costs $138,000. You qualify to "roll over" your gain because your "adjusted sales price" ($140,000 - $5,000 = $135,000) is lower than your purchase price ($138,000).

Remember, by rolling over the gain, you don't eliminate the tax; you only defer it. When you go to sell the new home, you'll either have to do another rollover or pay tax on all the gain from both residences. There are situations, however, in which you may qualify to eliminate altogether some of that gain.

Excluding Gain

Once you or your spouse have reached age 55, it is possible to completely exclude from tax up to $125,000 in gain on the sale of your primary residence. Not surprisingly, however, there are several important restrictions on this major tax break, and you are only allowed to claim it once in your life; it therefore is very important to consider carefully when to claim the exclusion in order to maximize your tax savings.

First, the home you sell must be your primary residence; vacation homes and rental property are not eligible for the exclusion. Next, the home must have been your primary residence for at least three out of the previous five years. Under certain circumstances, nursing-home occupancy can be counted for this purpose. You also must have owned your home for at least three out of the previous five years (although this need not be the same "three-out-of-five" that you occupied it). Finally, you must be at least 55 years old on the day you sell your home; turning 55 later in the same tax year will not qualify you for the exclusion.

> **Suggestion:** If you are close to turning 55, consider stipulating a settlement date after your 55th birthday in the sales contract

Married couples have one final restriction that applies to them. Since the exclusion is a once-in-a-lifetime opportunity, neither spouse can have claimed it previously. If your spouse was married once before, and the exclusion was claimed during that prior marriage, neither party to the current marriage is eligible to claim it. In short, the exclusion is available to married people only once per couple, not once per person.

> **Suggestion:** If you are contemplating marriage with a person who has already used the once-in-a-lifetime exclusion in a prior marriage and want to use the exclusion yourself, consider selling your home *before* you get married.

If you have never used your exclusion but are married to someone who has, you remain disqualified from claiming your exclusion only for as long as you remain married. If your spouse passes away or you subsequently divorce, you are again eligible to use your once-in-a-lifetime exclusion. (Don't get divorced just to claim the exclusion, though; IRS considers this a "sham transaction" and would disallow it!)

Also keep in mind that, as long as all the other requirements for the exclusion are met, only one of the two spouses needs to be 55 on the sale date in order to qualify for the exclusion. However, the younger spouse also will be considered to have used his or her once-in-a-lifetime exclusion, and will be ineligible to claim it again after turning 55.

A final strategy to consider: if you are selling a large family home to purchase a smaller residence, perhaps in a lower-cost area, it may make sense to combine the deferral of gain discussed above with the exclusion of gain explained here in order to maximize your tax savings

> **Example:** You are 60 years old. You purchased your home many years ago for $25,000. You sell it for $200,000, and immediately purchase a condominium in the Sun Belt for

$100,000. Your gain on this transaction is $175,000 ($200,000 - $25,000 = $175,000), which can be reduced by the once-in a lifetime exclusion to $50,000 ($175,000 - $125,000 = $50,000). Since the adjusted sales price of the old residence ($200,000 - $125,000 (exclusion) = $75,000) is less than the purchase price of the new one ($100,000), you also qualify to roll the $50,000 gain over into the new condominium. If you had not used the exclusion, your taxable gain would have been $100,000. Combining techniques saved you up to $28,000 in Federal taxes if you are in the 28% bracket ($100,000 x 28% = $28,000).

USING (AND ABUSING) YOUR HOME EQUITY

Your home may be an ideal source of tax-favored borrowing. In certain circumstances, the tax law allows you to deduct the interest you pay on a so-called "home equity loan" (i.e., a second mortgage secured by your primary residence). However, home equity loans are a double-edged sword. People who aren't careful in how they use their home equity can find themselves facing unexpected and expensive problems. Here's how to be "tax-smart" and "street-smart" with your home's equity.

First review the basic rules for deducting interest. Since the tax laws were reformed in 1986, most consumer interest is no longer deductible. Interest paid on credit card debts, student loans, car loans, and just about all other forms of unsecured consumer credit are no longer deductible.

Some other types of interest, however, are still deductible (usually within certain limits). Mortgages on your first and second home, investment interest, and business-related interest fall within the deductible category. So does one other type of interest: home equity interest.

In order to deduct the home equity interest you've paid, you must meet the following criteria: (1) you must itemize your deductions (i.e., file Schedule A) -- you can't use the deduction if you claim the standard deduction; (2) the loan on which you paid interest must be secured by your primary residence -- the lender must have a lien against your house; and, (3) the total outstanding indebtedness for which you claim the interest deduction cannot exceed $100,000.

Using your home's equity to meet your borrowing needs can provide some serious tax advantages. That's because interest you couldn't otherwise deduct can be claimed on your return if it's paid to satisfy a debt secured by your house. The planning opportunities are almost limitless. Consider just a few common possibilities:

Example 1: You want to purchase a new car. You can finance the car either through a car loan from your credit union or a home equity line from a local bank. Assuming the interest rates on both loans are about the same, your monthly payments will be about the same. You estimate those payments will be about $300 per month, and that in the first year you will pay $2,700 in interest (the rest will go to paying down the principal on the loan). The critical difference: interest on the credit union car loan isn't deductible. By opting for the tax-advantaged home equity loan, you can save $405 in Federal taxes if you are in the 15% tax bracket ($2,700 x 15% = $405), and over $750 if you're in the 28% bracket ($2,700 x 28% = $756).

Example 2: You have a $4,000 balance on your credit cards, and the interest rate is 19%. You can get a home equity loan that would bring the interest rate down to 8%, and your monthly payment down from $150 to $125. On top of this savings, however, the interest on your debt repayment becomes tax deductible, and you save about $180 in taxes for the first year if you're in the 15% bracket, and $336 in the 28% bracket.

Clearly, there can be some pleasant tax (and non-tax) advantages to borrowing against your home's equity: usually lower taxes and sometimes lower monthly loan payments. There are also risks if you misuse your home equity, risks that can leave you caught short further down the road. Although most of these risks relate to non-tax aspects of home equity loans, you should know how to avoid them. Here are a few simple rules:

First, don't get in over your head. Home equity loans frequently can be good ways of consolidating debts (especially high-rate credit card debts) or financing cars, but they should not be viewed as another source of "easy" credit. If you're the type of person who's inclined to "run up" large balances on your credit cards, you should think long and hard about a home equity loan. Running up a large balance against your home's equity could be a recipe for disaster. Defaulting on a home equity loan is not like defaulting on a credit card.

Because the loan is secured by your house, the lender can take action against it if you default, including foreclosure.

Before you tap into your home's equity, make sure there's a good purpose, a clear and short re-payment schedule, and adequate cash flow to make the monthly payments. Tax-smart use of equity loans should not be confused with a shopping spree you really can't afford!

Second, don't get in over your house's head. Lender's generally will only allow you to borrow a certain percentage of your house's value. For most lenders, that limit is 80%, although it sometimes can go as high as 85% or even 90%. Remember, this percentage, often referred to in lending shorthand as the "loan-to-value ratio" or "L-T-V ratio", includes all debts secured by your residence.

> **Example:** Your home is worth $100,000, and the balance of your mortgage is $50,000. If your lender has an 80% L-T-V limit, you can borrow up to $30,000 through a home equity loan ($100,000 x 80% = $80,000; $80,000 - $50,000 = $30,000).

The idea behind the L-T-V limits is to make sure that the total amount of debt secured by your house doesn't exceed its value. This way, if you default, the "equity cushion" between the amount your house is worth and the amount of debt outstanding against it assures your lenders of getting all their money back.

However, in today's climate of fluctuating real estate values, it's a good idea for you to monitor whether your L-T-V limit is consistent with changing market realities. After all, you need to protect your "equity cushion" at least as much as the bank does. If you had to move, for example, you'd need that equity for a down-payment on a new house. Or, perhaps you're approaching retirement and your equity is part of your nest egg. If you've "maxxed out" on home equity borrowing, and market values in your area drop just a little bit, you may not have enough equity to meet your other needs.

Next, don't get in too long. If you anticipate moving in the not-too-distant future, be very careful with using your home's equity. Your going to need that money to buy a new house, but it won't be available if there's still a balance on your home equity loan when its time to sell. Lenders have rules about re-payment schedules, and these rules are usually tied to the size of your loan. Make sure, however, that your re-payment schedule fits in with your plans, and not just the bank's. And remember, the longer you take to pay back your home equity loan, the more interest the bank earns from you.

Finally, keep track of the paperwork. A home equity loan is a secured line of credit. This means that the bank files a lien against your house. Once the loan is paid off, be certain the lender has completed the paperwork to get the lien released. This can save you time and hassles when you go to sell your house later. Because home equity loans are usually revolving lines of credit (i.e., you can tap into them as needed), be confident that you will have no future need to borrow against your equity before you ask the lender to close out your account. Remember, though: just because you pay your loan down to zero does not mean the lender will automatically release its lien against your house.

MAXIMIZE TAX-DEFERRED RETIREMENT SAVINGS

There are several forms of retirement savings sanctioned by the tax law. In order to encourage people to save for their own retirements, all of these plans traditionally have provided tremendous tax incentives. These incentives are even greater with the new higher tax rates created by OBRA 93.

If your retirement plan does not allow you to contribute to the savings, as with many employers' pensions, one of its main tax advantages is the ability of plan assets to earn income on a pre-tax basis. The interest, dividends and/or capital gains your retirement savings earn are not taxed to you until you receive them. (How they are taxed when you do receive them is discussed later in this Chapter, in the section on retirement plan withdrawals). This in essence means that money which would otherwise go to pay taxes on the assets' income can stay in your account. This tax-free compounding of interest increases the value of your account dramatically over time.

> **Example:** If you invest $5,000 to earn 8% simple taxable interest for 20 years, at the end of that period you would have a total of $18,638 if you are in the 15% tax bracket and only $15,325 if you are in the 28% bracket. By contrast, a retirement plan containing $5,000 earning 8% would be worth $23,305 after 20 years.

Of even greater significance, if the plan is a qualified plan (and, for rank-and-file employees, most are), the money your employer sets aside on your behalf is not considered income to you until you withdraw it from your account. Meanwhile, your employer is allowed to claim an immediate deduction for the amounts it contributes. This is a major exception to traditional tax rules, which wouldn't allow an employer to claim a deduction for such contributions until its employee recognizes them in income. This makes qualified retirement plans very attractive for employers and employees.

If your retirement plan does allow you to contribute, such as in a 401(k) plan, in addition to all of the benefits above, you have the opportunity to shelter some of your own income from taxation. Within limits, you can make contributions out of your own salary to such plans, and your income for the year is reduced by the amount of the contributions. These plans truly are among the best deals going anywhere in the tax law.

Clearly, there are substantial benefits to be found in tax-favored retirement savings. It therefore is in your interest to be "socking away" into retirement savings the maximum amount your budget can possibly afford. Putting aside the maximum amount available (or allowable under the law) can save you hundreds or even thousands off your annual tax bill. At the same time, you'll be helping yourself prepare for an increasingly uncertain future.

Of course, in order to enjoy the benefits of tax-advantaged retirement savings, you must comply with a very complex set of rules. Experts make careers out of interpreting and explaining the rules relating to retirement plans, so only a very broad outline can be presented here. However, the discussion that follows should provide you with enough information to know which forms of tax-advantaged retirement savings are best for you.

Retirement Plans for Employees

Non-contributory Plans. Many retirement plans available to employees are non-contributory. That is, your employer makes a contribution based on your salary, and perhaps your age and/or years of employment. As discussed above, the advantage of these plans to you is that you are receiving tax-deferred income and that such income is growing on a tax-deferred basis. In exchange for these benefits, the tax law expects you not to start drawing on these assets until you retire.

There are two traditional types of retirement plans. The first type promises to pay you a certain percentage of your salary when you retire. The company makes this promise to its workforce, and then places as much or as little into its retirement plan as its actuaries say is needed to meet this promise. Since your employer is promising to pay you a specific benefit, say 60% of your salary at retirement, this type of plan is called a "defined benefit" plan.

Under the other common type of retirement plan, your employer promises to place in its retirement account a certain percentage of your annual earnings. Since the employer commits to how much it will put in on your behalf, and not how much it will pay out, these plans are known as "defined contribution" plans. Defined contribution plans can be based on a fixed percentage of income, or they can vary each year depending on the firm's profits. The former type of plan is called a "money purchase" defined contribution plan, and the latter a "profit sharing" defined contribution plan. Annual contributions to a money purchase plan are mandatory. Profit sharing contributions are optional, but must be made at least once every three or so years.

Under both defined benefit and defined contribution plans, there are limits as to how much your employer can pay into a retirement plan on your behalf. In the case of defined benefit plans, the most your employer can set aside each year is enough money to fund a retirement benefit equal to either $115,641 (indexed for inflation) or 100% of your salary (averaged over its three highest years), whichever is less. For defined contribution plans, each year your employer generally can set aside up to 25% of your salary (to a maximum of $30,000) in a money purchase plan, and up to 15% of your salary (again to $30,000) in a profit sharing plan. Of course, in the case of any retirement plan, your employer can choose to provide lower benefits, and many do.

Your employer can require you to work for a certain period of time before the funds it sets aside on your behalf become your nonforfeitable property. This is called "vesting". There are two different approaches to vesting, gradual and all-at-once. If your employer phases-in your vesting, it usually must start to do so by the third year in which you are covered by the plan, and finish doing so by the seventh. If your employer chooses all-at-once vesting, it can wait until the fifth year you are covered by the plan to do so. Sometimes these vesting periods are even shorter when the plan covers too many "highly-compensated employees". Also, your employer can usually wait up to six months from your hire date before it starts covering you under its plan.

The tax law contains a host of other rules regarding retirement plans. If the employer fails to satisfy these rules, the plan loses its "qualified" status, and all of the tax advantages described above are lost -- for both the employer and the employee. Clearly, this is a disastrous result all around.

If you are covered by either a defined benefit or a defined contribution plan, it is important for you to understand how to treat any disbursements you receive from such plans. These disbursements are called "withdrawals", and the penalties for doing the wrong thing with a withdrawal can be very high. Again, review the section on retirement plan withdrawals later in this Chapter to avoid the pitfalls to be found in this complicated area.

If you work for a small business, you may be covered by a streamlined form of retirement plan known as an "SEP", or "Simplified Employee Pension". SEPs allow small employers to avoid the intricate rules just described by in essence making annual contributions to their employees' IRAs (Individual Retirement Accounts). Among other things, SEPs dramatically lower the cost of administering retirement plans. This is a good part of the reason they are popular with small business owners. Additionally, an employer can decide on a year-by-year basis whether and by how much to fund its SEP contributions.

In exchange for this simplicity, SEPs follow a fairly uniform set of rules. The maximum amount your employer can contribute to a SEP IRA on your behalf is 15% of your salary (up to $30,000). Your employer can require you to work for three years before including you in its SEP program. However, if you are over 21, earn more than $300 per year, and have met this service requirement, your employer must cover you in its SEP.

If you are covered by a SEP, it is important for you to understand that, once funds are placed in your SEP IRA, they are yours. They cannot be reclaimed at some later date by your employer. From that moment forward, the account is treated like any other IRA. The rules regarding IRAs are discussed later in this section.

Contributory Plans. If your employer offers a contributory retirement plan, it is essential tax planning that you make the maximum possible contributions to such a plan. 401(k) plans, named after the section of the tax law that created them, are the most common form of such plans. These plans usually allow you to designate a certain percentage of each paycheck to be deposited into an account on your behalf. The amount of income you pay tax on each year is reduced by the amount you put into your 401(k) account. The tax law allows you to defer a maximum of $8,994 (indexed for inflation) in income each year. Some plans have lower limits if they cover too many "highly compensated employees".

> **Example:** You are married and earn $48,000 per year, placing you and your spouse in the 28% tax bracket. You are paid a gross amount of $2,000 semi-monthly. Your employer offers a 401(k) plan to its employees. If you were to elect to participate in the plan by deferring 5% of your income, $100 per pay period ($2,000 x 5% = $100) would be placed in your 401(k) account. This would reduce your taxable income by $2,400 that year ($100 x 24 = $2,400), saving you $672 in taxes ($2,400 x 28% = $672). By the same token, because you're not paying tax on the amount being deferred, your actual take-home pay would only go down about $80 as a result of your $100 deferral (the actual amount depends on your withholding rate, your spouse's withholding and some other factors).

Of course, as with any form of qualified retirement plan, the funds in your 401(k) account accumulate interest and dividends on a tax-deferred basis. This adds even further to the value of your savings.

If you work for a small business, again the tax law provides a mechanism allowing your employer to make the option of deferring income available to its employees. These plans are called SARSEPs (Salary Reduction SEPs). They operate basically the same way that 401(k)s do, but on a simplified scale. As an employee, you still get all of the advantages of deferring income described above. Not many small businesses have taken advantage of SARSEPs; if yours hasn't, it should.

Sometimes, your employer will "match" all or part of the contributions you elect to defer. This means that, up to a certain percentage, for every dollar you contribute, your employer will fully or partially match your contribution. Over a period of time, these matching contributions become your non-forfeitable property. Matching increases the value of your contributions in two ways. First, it is a tax-deferred source of additional income. Your employer is giving you more money, but you don't pay tax on it until it's withdrawn. Second, as always, the amounts your employer contribute earn interest and dividends on a tax-deferred basis. At an absolute minimum, you should contribute to your employer's 401(k) plan as much as your employer will match. If you don't you're basically turning down free money.

The funds placed in 401(k) accounts often are managed by brokerage houses or securities firms. These firms usually provide a family of mutual funds in which to invest your assets. Choosing from among these funds is not an easy task, but here are a few thoughts to consider. First, be sure you diversify. Spread your 401(k) money over three funds (if that many are offered). You may want to vary the degree of risk slightly, placing a small amount in more aggressive funds. If you do this, you might consider balancing it out by allocating a small percentage of your account to a fund that invests in government securities. Always make choices that are consistent with your overall risk tolerance.

Second, make choices that are appropriate for your stage in life. Younger employees should choose investments that emphasize capital growth, while those nearing retirement should seek funds that offer both income and security of principal. The firm managing your company's 401(k) can provide you with descriptions of all of the choices available to you. Read these materials carefully before deciding what to do with your funds.

Other Plans. Certain groups of employees have unique retirement plans available only to them. These groups include government employees, educational institution employees, and employees of other non-profit organizations. It is not possible to discuss here the special rules that apply to these types of plans. If you are covered by such a plan, remember the general principle discussed above: contribute as much as you possibly can to any plan that allows you to defer income on a pre-tax basis.

Retirement Plans for the Self-employed

If you are self-employed, your retirement planning options are slightly more limited than those discussed so far. The plans discussed above are only available to corporations, although the tax law contains parallel plans to cover your situation. The major difference in self-employed retirement plans is that they do not distinguish between employer and employee contributions. The tax law treats a self-employed person as both an employer and an employee for retirement plan purposes. The net effect of this restriction is to lower the amount of money self-employed people can set aside in retirement savings each year.

The two basic options available to self-employed individuals are SEPs and Keogh plans. Self-employed SEPs function in much the same ways as the employer SEPs described above, except that the maximum contribution percentage is lowered from 15% to approximately 13.04% Once the funds are placed in a self-employed person's SEP IRA, they are treated as any other IRA. As a self-employed person, you can establish a SARSEP for the benefit of any employees you may have, but the total contribution to your account still cannot exceed 13.04%.

Keogh plans permit self-employed persons to establish and

maintain defined benefit and defined contribution plans in much the same fashion as those discussed above. The advantage to these plans is that they allow self-employed people to defer more of their income into retirement savings than SEPs do. The higher contribution limits applicable to money purchase defined contribution plans and to defined benefit plans can be used when establishing a Keogh (with some technical adjustments). The disadvantage is that they are more complex to administer, and likely will require the assistance of a pension expert.

One other advantage to SEPs is that contributions can be made anytime up until the return is due, including extensions. This provides you with the flexibility to do some late tax planning, deciding as late as April (or August if you extend your return) of 19X2 how much you want to contribute to a SEP for 19X1 and deduct on your 19X1 tax return. Keoghs, by contrast, allow deductions up until the due date of the return (without extensions), but only if the plan was in existence before the tax year in question closed. In short, Keoghs provide more limited opportunities for after-the-fact tax planning than do SEPs.

If you are a high-income self-employed person, consider consulting with a pension plan administrator to see if a Keogh can be of benefit to you. If you are still a struggling entrepreneur, the SEP probably is a better bet for you right now.

Individual Retirement Accounts

By now, most Americans are familiar with the term IRA, or Individual Retirement Account. Before the last major overhaul of the tax laws in 1986, IRAs were a wonderful form of both tax-deductible and tax-advantaged savings. The deduction is a lot more limited now, but there are still benefits to be found in IRAs.

Since 1986, IRAs have come in two varieties: deductible and non-deductible. Whether or not you can deduct IRA contributions depends on whether you (or your spouse) are covered by an employer's plan, and, if so, how much you make. Regardless of whether or not you can deduct your IRA contributions, IRA contributions still can grow in the account on a tax-deferred basis. As was seen in the first example above, this benefit can make even non-deductible IRAs attractive (more on this later).

Contribution Amounts. IRA contributions are limited to a maximum of $2,000 per person per year (you can contribute less). If you make less than $2,000, you can only contribute to an IRA up to the amount of your actual earnings. If you have earnings that entitle you to make an IRA contribution, there is a $200 minimum on IRA contributions; if your earnings are less than $200, you still may contribute this amount.

If you have a non-working spouse, he or she is also entitled to make an IRA contribution, up to a maximum of $250. You and your spouse can divide up the amounts you contribute between accounts however you choose, but you cannot put more than $2,000 in one person's account in any year.

> **Example:** You earn $30,000 per year and are not covered by an employer's retirement plan. Your spouse does not work. You can make a maximum IRA contribution of $2,250. However, only $2,000 of this amount can be titled in your name (or your spouse's). Below this limit, you can split the deduction into your accounts any way you wish (e.g., $1,125 to you and $1,125 to your spouse).

Deductibility. As was suggested above, the deductibility of IRA contributions depends on outside pension coverage, and then on income. If you (or your spouse if you are married) are covered by a pension, your contribution is only fully deductible if your income is beneath certain limits. Once your income crosses the applicable limit, your deduction gets phased out, until it is eliminated for incomes $10,000 or more above the limit. The limit is $25,000 if you are a single filer or head of household, $40,000 if you file jointly with your spouse, and $0 if you and your spouse file separately. Thus, you cannot claim any IRA deduction if you (or your spouse) are covered by an employer plan and your income exceeds, $35,000, $50,000, and $10,000, respectively.

Partial contributions are computed based on the amount by which your income exceeds the limits (within the $10,000 phase-out range).

> **Example:** You are single, and have income of $31,000. You are covered by your employer's pension. This puts your income $6,000 over the limit applicable to you ($31,000 - $25,000 = $6,000). This makes the maximum $2,000 IRA contribution 60% non-deductible ($6,000/ $10,000 = 60%), and 40% deductible. Thus, any amount you contribute up to $800 is deductible($2,000 x 40% = $800), but any contribution above $800 (and under the $2,000 maximum) is non-deductible.

You are considered covered by an employer's plan if at any time during the year you or your spouse were eligible to participate in such a plan, whether or not you chose to do so. It also doesn't matter whether or not your benefits have vested; once you are on the plan's books, you are considered covered. As a practical matter, the way to tell if you are covered by an employer's plan is to review your W-2. If either of the two little squares in Box 6 of that form (labelled "Pension Plan" and "Deferred Compensation") is checked, you are covered by your employer's plan.

You may find the decision tree on the next page helpful in determining the deductibility of your IRA contributions.

Self-employeds. For self-employed persons, you are subject to the rules limiting deductibility of IRA contributions if you've established a Keogh plan or if you make a SEP contribution for the year in question. Since SEP contributions are based on net income, a self-employed person with marginal net income may be better off foregoing a SEP for the year and claiming an IRA instead. Of course, you must meet all the usual IRA requirements in order to qualify for the deduction, and, more importantly, you must be able to afford the contribution.

IRA Deductibility Decision-Tree:

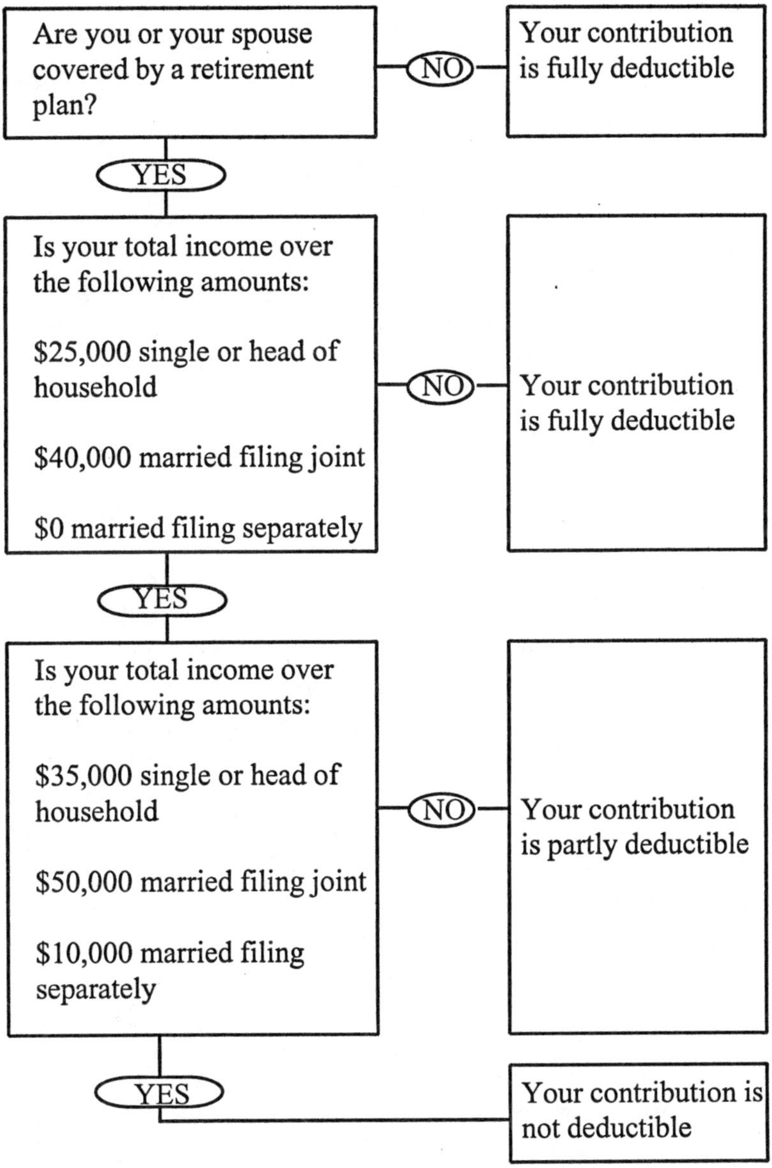

Example: You began a computer consulting business this year. Your net income for the year was only $2,000. You would be entitled to make a maximum SEP contribution of approximately $240 (the actual formula for determining SEP contributions requires you to subtract from your income 1/2 of the FICA tax you paid, making the computation a little complex). You are in the 15% tax bracket, so this would result in a tax savings of only $36 ($240 x 15% = $36). Alternatively, you could make an IRA contribution of $2,000, which would produce a tax savings of $300. Assuming you can only afford one option or the other, the IRA is the better choice for this year.

Sometimes, it may be advantageous to combine a SEP and a deductible IRA contribution, in order to maximize tax savings (assuming you have the resources to pay for such contributions).

Example: You are a self-employed landscaper. You just started your business last year, and your net business income for 1993 is only $5,000. Your husband is an administrative assistant for a large corporation. He makes $32,000 annually, and is covered by his employer's pension plan. You have no other sources of income.

You have several options in this situation. First, you could make a SEP contribution of approximately $600. Since you and your husband are in the 15% tax bracket, this saves you $90 off your 1993 tax bill ($600 x 15% = $90).

Instead, however, you could forego the SEP and make the maximum allowable IRA contribution. Since you and your husband have combined income of under $40,000, this contribution would be fully deductible. Thus, a contribution of $2,000 would net you a tax savings of $300.

There are even more possibilities. You could make both a deductible SEP and a deductible IRA contribution, since you qualify for both. Or, if you have the means to support such a strategy, you and your husband could both make deductible IRA contributions, and you could make a de ductible SEP contribution. This would result in combined retirement savings of $4,600 ($2,000 IRA + $2,000 IRA + $600 SEP = $4,600) and tax savings of $690 ($300 + $300 + $90 = $690).

Non-deductible IRAs. If you don't qualify to make deductible IRA contributions, this does not automatically mean that you should dismiss the IRA option. If you choose to make a non-deductible contribution, your IRA continues to earn income on a tax-deferred basis. Many financial advisors therefore think non-deductible IRAs are a good deal.

However, some professionals believe that the restrictions placed on IRA accounts outweigh their benefits once the ability to deduct contributions is lost. For example, unless you're willing to pay a 10% penalty tax, you can't withdraw your IRA funds until age 59-1/2. By contrast, if you took those IRA funds and invested them in a tax-free municipal bond fund, you would achieve the same tax results and still have access to your money whenever you needed it.

There is something to be said for this latter argument. There's also something to be said for "locking up" your funds until retirement in an IRA, especially if you're not a strong saver. Also, IRAs give you more diverse investment choices than municipal bond funds. This can be a close call, and you should weigh both arguments to decide which fits better with your spending habits, financial discipline, and overall outlook.

Due Dates. IRA contributions must be deposited by the due date of your return. If you file early, you still have until April 15th to get the money in the account, though.

PUT YOUR LIFE INSURANCE TO WORK

Buying permanent life insurance (e.g., whole life, universal life, variable life) offers savvy investors the opportunity for several tax breaks. Understanding the tax rules can help you make the most of your existing policies, and should assist you in planning for additional insurance investments.

Foremost, just as with term insurance (e.g., the group life coverage provided by your employer), the death benefit paid by permanent insurance is free from income tax. (Remember, though, the death benefit usually is part of your "gross estate" for estate tax purposes. Tax strategies for handling the estate tax are discussed in another section of this Chapter.) There are some other important advantages unique to permanent insurance, however, that you should understand.

First, permanent insurance offers a form of tax-advantaged savings. While it would be inappropriate to view insurance exclusively as an investment, one of the appealing aspects of permanent insurance is its ability to build-up a cash value. Some people even treat their permanent insurance as a form of "forced savings" because of this feature. Adding to the incentive, the cash value on your insurance earns interest free of Federal income taxes. Over time, this tax-free compounding of interest can result in significantly increased savings.

> **Example:** If you invest $5,000 to earn 4% simple taxable interest for 5 years, at the end of that period you would have a total of $5,910 if you are in the 15% tax bracket and only $5,765 if you are in the 28% bracket. By contrast, a life insurance policy with $5,000 in accumulated cash value earning a guaranteed rate of 4% would return $6,085 after 5 years.

When considering the tax advantages of insurance, bear in mind that some forms of permanent insurance can earn more than the minimum rate guaranteed. Also keep in mind that, as more time passes, the benefits of tax free income compound; this in essence means that the "spread" between taxable and non-taxable returns increases with time.

There's one final tax advantage associated with permanent insurance, but it is a tactic that should be deployed cautiously. It can save you money, but if abused has the potential to leave your beneficiaries without adequate insurance coverage. Here's how the concept works: almost all permanent life insurance contracts allow policyholders to borrow against their cash value, subject to some restrictions, discussed below. As long as these restrictions are satisfied, the loan is tax free to the policyholder. Moreover, the loan need not ever be repaid; the outstanding loan balance is simply subtracted from the death benefit the insurance company pays your beneficiary when you die. In fact, if you want, you don't even have to pay interest on the loan; as interest accrues, the insurance company simply adds it to the loan balance. In essence, the loan becomes "tax free"!

> **Example:** You own a whole life insurance policy with a $100,000 cash value in which your spouse is your sole beneficiary. Several years ago, you borrowed $5,000 against your cash value in order to pay for home improvements. You never made repayments of principal or interest on your loan, and at the time of your death the loan balance had grown to $7,000. Your spouse would receive a death benefit of $93,000 ($100,000 - $7,000).

The restrictions on policy loans mentioned above are full of legal technicalities, so you'd be well advised to talk to your agent or broker about the details as they apply to your particular policy. In general, the law imposes limits on the percentage of the total cash value you are allowed to borrow. The limits are too complex to explain here, but you can figure on never being allowed to borrow more than half your cash value (and usually less). Failure to meet these requirements results in immediate taxation of all deferred income. Your insurance company isn't likely to let you run afoul of these tests, but, again, talk to your agent or broker before acting.

There is an important and obvious downside to borrowing against your life insurance: if you borrow too much, you'll leave your loved ones under-protected, thwarting the original purpose of your insurance planning. The restrictions in the tax law limiting how much you can borrow usually, but not always, protect against this, but you should weigh your options carefully before making any major decisions. The primary purpose of life insurance coverage, after all, must always be to provide for those you would prematurely leave behind. Thus, this technique is usually most appropriate for older people who have owned their policies for many years and have less of a need for a large death benefit. However, in unusual circumstances, almost anyone can benefit from using it. Although the decision to tap into your life insurance's cash value should never be taken lightly, this is an important tool that can be an effective part of your overall financial planning.

MINIMIZE THE ESTATE TAX BITE

The old saw regarding death and taxes gets a new lease on life when discussion turns to the Federal estate tax. For certain individuals, life's two most dreaded events can combine to provide a one-two punch that leaves their survivors breathless. The typical scenario: you've worked all your life, provided for your family's future, and gone onto your eternal reward. If you've left too many worldly goods and material possessions behind, the law imposes a tax on your net worth before any of it can be received by the objects of your bounty. What's worse, the rates at which the Federal estate tax is levied can reach a whopping 55%!

Generally, if your net worth -- or your combined net worth if you are married -- exceeds $600,000, or if it is likely to reach that threshold before you die, you need to be concerned about the Federal estate tax. Some interesting items go into computing your net worth, too -- things many people wouldn't expect. The law says that all your assets are included in the computation, and they do mean all: your houses, cars, bank account and investment account balances, CDs, stocks, bonds, and collectibles are all obvious components of your net worth. But you may be surprised to learn that insurance proceeds from policies you own and retirement account balances from IRAs, SEPs, 401(k)s, Keoghs, and employer pensions are also included in your net worth. When you add these assets into the equation, it is not hard to see that more people than expected have to worry about the Federal estate tax; a house that's paid off, some life insurance, a solid pension plan, a little nest egg in the bank, and that magical $600,000 figure can quickly start closing in!

> **Example:** You and your spouse have just entered your retirement years. You have lived in the same home for almost 30 years, and have seen inflation increase its value to approximately $200,000. The mortgage has been paid off for several years now. You have $75,000 in paid-up life insurance, and your spouse has $25,000. You maintain $5,000 in a checking account, $20,000 in a savings account, and also own two $50,000 CDs. You have partici

> pated for many years in a company-sponsored pension plan, and the value of your pension is currently almost $140,000. Your spouse also has a small retirement plan worth approximately $30,000. Additionally, you both have a total of about $20,000 in IRA accounts. Excluding the value of any personal property or collectibles you may own, your combined net worth for Federal estate tax purposes is $615,000. You may very well "spend down" your net worth below the $600,000 estate tax threshold. However, if you and your spouse were both to pass away unexpectedly tomorrow, your estate could owe up to $5,550 in Federal taxes. Through proper estate planning, these taxes can be avoided at a fraction of that cost.

If you think you may have estate tax concerns, there are things you can do to minimize or even eliminate the Federal estate tax bite. If, for example, you are married and your combined net worth is under $1.2 million but is still over the $600,000 threshold, there are steps you can take to eliminate Federal estate taxes altogether. The rest of this section will be devoted to this and other techniques for handling estate taxes.

However, estate planning is <u>not</u> an area for do-it-yourselfers; the rules are too complicated and the stakes are too high. Moreover, you almost certainly will require an attorney to draft the legal documents necessary to employ the techniques described here. If you sense the Federal estate tax may affect you, read on to become familiar with the terrain, but by all means seek competent professional assistance in designing and implementing an appropriate estate plan!

One final note before diving in: throughout this discussion, you've seen the term "Federal" estate tax. That's because most states have some form of death taxes of their own, separate and apart from the Federal levies. These taxes vary widely from state to state, and are much harder to plan around; the rates are also much, much lower for state death taxes than for the Federal estate tax. They therefore usually are not the primary goal of estate planning. In this discussion, the focus is only on Federal estate taxes.

Annual Gifts

One technique for minimizing estate taxes involves annual gift-giving. When you give money or other property away, it's obviously no longer yours. Therefore, in most situations, it's not considered part of your net worth for Federal estate tax purposes.

Notice the phrase "most situations" in that last sentence. Believe it or not, some of the gifts people give to their relatives and friends -- maybe some of the gifts you have given -- are potentially subject to Federal Gift Tax either because of how they were given or because of how much was given. In order to get some understanding of how this all works, first review the general rule, and then consider its exceptions.

In general, the law allows you to give away up to $10,000 dollars (cash or property) per recipient per year free of Federal tax. If you are married, you and your spouse can each give away this amount, i.e., up to $20,000. In fact, you can give away the whole amount yourself, and your spouse's allowance will be attributed to you (assuming he or she doesn't use it).

Now for a discussion of the exceptions. First, if you give more than $10,000 to one person in a year (or more than a total of $20,000 if you are married), the excess theoretically is taxable. In practice, however, you reduce your $600,000 estate tax exemption by the excess amount.

> **Example:** You are single, and give your grandchild $15,000 in 19X1. You must file a gift tax return by April 15, 19X2. This will reduce your estate tax exemption by $5,000 (the excess over the $10,000 annual allowance), to $595,000.
>
> **Suggestion:** To avoid this problem, give your grandchild $10,000 in 19X1 and the other $5,000 on January 1, 19X2.

The second exception relates to certain gifts made within three years of death. Generally such gifts follow the usual gift tax rules discussed above, and are not taken into account when computing your estate tax liability. However, in a few very technical situations, when the gift comes with "strings attached" (i.e., if you retain some interest in it or some right to control it), it can be counted in your net worth for computing the Federal estate tax.

By now you may have noticed that the estate and gift taxes seem to have a lot of overlap. That's because several years ago Congress decided to integrate the two taxes to cut down on some aggressive tax planning activities. This means that there is now great interplay between estate taxes and gift taxes. As a result, people who may be concerned about the estate tax have to be mindful of the gift tax when doing their estate planning. Conversely, people making gifts sometimes have to be certain there are no estate tax consequences to their proposed transactions. It can get pretty confusing, but as long as you keep below $10,000 per person per year on gifts and stay below $600,000 on your net worth, you are in the clear. Again, when you cross these thresholds, it's time to seek professional advice.

To add to the confusion, the amount of tax you actually pay depends on whether you've previously made taxable gifts; in this sense, the gift tax is cumulative. Therefore, the more taxable gifts you make, the higher your gift tax rate becomes for each subsequent gift. It therefore is important to be sure and take maximum advantage of the $10,000 annual allowance.

Now that you understand the basics of the annual gift tax allowance, consider some strategies for deploying it effectively to minimize estate taxes. The annual exclusion is often an ideal solution to potential estate tax problems for people whose net worth is right on the border of the $600,000 threshold.

> **Example:** Consider the couple discussed at the beginning of this section whose net worth was $615,000. By making a gift of $6,000 to each of their three grandchildren, for example, they can bring their net worth under $600,000 and avoid Federal estate taxes.
>
> **Suggestion:** This couple should periodically review its

finances to see if they again creep over the $600,000 threshold. If they do, gifts may again be the solution to their problems.

Even if your high net worth puts you well within the estate tax regime, you can still make good use of the $10,000 annual allowance to minimize your problems. Consider these examples:

Example 1: You and your spouse have two married children. In one year, if you so desired, you and your spouse could remove $80,000 from your net worth tax free, simply by both giving $10,000 to each of your four "children" (2 spouses x $10,000 x 4 children = $80,000).

Example 2: Same facts as above, but your two married children each have two children. Now, if you want to, in one year you can shrink your net worth by $160,000 (2 spouses x $10,000 x 8 children/grandchildren = $160,000).

Example 3: Suppose you want to use the $10,000 allowance to reduce your net worth and minimize estate taxes, but are reluctant to make such drastic adjustments as in the examples above. After all, you may need that money at some point. Set up you own annual gifting program, using a more gradual approach. Give each of your four grandchildren $2,500 a year; after 5 years, you will have incrementally removed $50,000 from your net worth (4 grandchildren x $2,500 x 5 years = $50,000).

Suggestion: If you adopt the annual approach discussed in Example 3, don't be afraid to change it. If you decide finances are becoming tight, pull back to $1,000 or $2,000 per grandchild per year. If you realize you may have been too conservative in your original projections, you can always raise the gifts to $5,000 or $6,000 per year. Just don't go over that magical $10,000 figure!

Warning: If you decide to adopt the annual approach discussed in Example 3, remember to plan carefully for your future needs. Even though your net worth may be over $600,000, it's probable that a large percentage of that is in illiquid assets -- your house, life insurance, retirement plans. Your gifts probably will have to come from your liquid assets, such as savings accounts, money markets, CDs. Be sure you don't make yourself cash poor when you start making annual gifts.

Now that you have some idea how much to give and when to give it, you still must decide what to give -- cash, stocks, bonds, a favorite auto? As was suggested above, it is important that you retain enough cash to keep yourself liquid throughout your golden years. However, most other property -- stocks, bonds, real estate, vintage autos -- usually should be received by inheritance rather than lifetime gift. The tax laws provide a strong preference for inheriting appreciated property: any appreciation you've accumulated in them is erased when you die. Your beneficiaries inherit them at their full market value. This powerful incentive does not apply to lifetime gifts; your appreciation in such transfers "carries over" to the recipient, and he or she must pay income tax on all that gain when the asset is subsequently sold.

Example: You own stock worth $10,000. You bought the stock many years ago for only $1,000. If you were to sell the stock, there would be a $9,000 taxable gain. If you give this stock to your child, and he or she sells it, there would still be a $9,000 taxable gain. However, if you gave the child $10,000 in cash and left the stock to your child in a will, that $9,000 gain would be erased upon your death.

On the other hand, in some situations it can actually be advantageous to give away property instead of cash. This technique works well for people who own assets they know are going to appreciate considerably in value before they die. If the math works, it can make more tax sense to transfer the asset sooner rather than later. Doing so removes the appreciation from one's net worth.

Example: You own stock in a company that consistently appreciates in value at an average rate of 10% per year.

> Your investment in this company is currently worth $500,000. If you live another 15 years, this stock should be worth $2.1 million (based on its past performance). By gifting the stock to your heirs now, the $1.6 million in anticipated appreciation over the next 15 years is removed from your net worth when you die, saving you hundreds of thousands in Federal estate taxes.

Keep in mind, however, that this technique almost always applies to people with very high net worths who are already certain of paying estate taxes. Moreover, using this approach is always part of a carefully (and professionally) drafted estate plan. For most people who do not have a high net worth, the general rule should be: whenever possible, give cash instead of property, and always seek professional advice before giving away during your lifetime property that has substantially appreciated in value.

There's one last tax-free gift-giving opportunity that many people are not aware of: gifts of educational or medical payments. You may directly pay the medical expenses of another person, including medical insurance, without limit, and still not pay gift tax. The same thing applies to expenses paid directly to an educational organization for tuition (but not room and board). You don't have to worry about the $10,000 limit; it doesn't apply, and the amount you pay isn't counted against it. In fact, you don't even have to file a gift tax return. Just be sure to write the check directly to the institution or provider, and not to the person on whose behalf you're making the payment.

A final reminder regarding annual gifts: in the process of trying to reduce or eliminate your taxable estate, don't leave yourself financially "short". Remember, in order to get money out of your estate, you more or less need to give up all future claims on it. Make sure you've left yourself with enough to enjoy your golden years in comfort and security!

The Marital Deduction

Another essential estate planning tool, available to married couples, is known as the marital deduction. The marital deduction is unlimited, which means that you can give as much as you want to your spouse, while you're living or through your will when you die, and not pay gift or estate tax on it.

> **Example 1:** You own 50 acres of undeveloped land worth $100,000. You transfer title to this land to your wife. You do not owe any gift tax on this transaction.

> **Example 2:** When you die, your net worth is $700,000. You leave $350,000 to your spouse, and $350,000 to be divided among your three children. Since the first $350,000 goes to your spouse tax free (thanks to the unlimited marital deduction), the amount of your taxable estate is reduced to $350,000. Since the estate tax threshold is $600,000, your estate does not owe any Federal estate taxes, saving your beneficiaries up to $37,000!

Example 2 illustrates the beauty of the unlimited marital deduction: through careful use, it can allow married couples to double their estate tax threshold from $600,000 to $1.2 million.

> **Example:** Same facts as in Example 2 above, except your net worth is $1.2 million. You leave $600,000 to your spouse, and $600,000 to be divided among your three children. The first $600,000 passes to your spouse free of Federal estate tax, and the next $600,000 just misses the estate tax threshold. You've saved up to $192,800 in Federal estate taxes!

If you think about it, this approach only makes sense. Since you and your spouse each get a $600,000 estate tax exemption, combining them through the marital deduction effectively allows you to double your tax planning power.

This technique is not without its difficulties, however. Consider the last example as a case in point. Your surviving spouse received $600,000 from you; however, he or she probably owns some assets individually. He or she now has a net worth over $600,000, and no spouse with which to take advantage of the marital deduction. If your combined net worth is over $1.2 million, you cannot completely avoid this problem; you will need to consider a combination of estate planning techniques to deal with your situation.

However, Many couples who have estate tax problems fall within the $600,000 to $1.2 million range; with a little planning, they can avoid Federal estate taxes altogether. It may require re-titling some assets from one spouse to another, or into or out of joint ownership, and will definitely require carefully prepared wills. Among other concerns, you need to be sure that your individual net worths are roughly equivalent, so that the second spouse to pass away does not leave too large an estate. As the examples above make clear, however, the tax savings for these efforts will pay for themselves many times over!

Example: You and your spouse jointly own your home, worth $300,000. You each own a CD worth $100,000 (total value of both CDs is $200,000). You also individually own an investment portfolio worth $400,000. Your combined net worth is $900,000. If you are the first to pass away, your spouse automatically receives your interest in your house, the value of which is $150,000. This leaves you with $500,000 in other assets ($100,000 CD + $400,000 investment portfolio = $500,000), for a total net worth of $650,000. While you may have a minor estate tax problem, you can quickly see that your surviving spouse could have a big one. Suppose you left the $400,000 portfolio to your children and the $100,000 CD to your spouse? You've avoided estate taxes, but your spouse is now "house poor". Instead, you could leave the investment portfolio to your spouse and the CD to your children. Now your spouse has adequate resources to live out his or her years comfortably, but also has a net worth of $800,000. What can you do?

Suggestion: Re-title half of the assets in the investment portfolio separately in your spouse's name, and leave your share of the portfolio assets along with your CD to your children. Now, if you die first, your surviving spouse has adequate assets to live on (her CD and her share of the re-titled portfolio assets), and you have avoided Federal estate tax. If your spouse makes identical provisions in his or her will, you still will pay no estate taxes if you end up being the second to die.

If you are concerned that giving a large portion of your estate to your children will financially strap your surviving spouse, consider placing the children's share in a trust. Under the trust, you can give your surviving spouse limited rights to receive income from the trust in case of "hardship", and then direct that the assets be distributed to your children upon your wife's death. If it's drafted properly, the trust protects your surviving spouse in an emergency, but still gets those assets out of his or her estate and to your children.

Example: Consider the example above, where it was suggested you could re-title assets in order to facilitate maximum usage of the marital deduction. Another possible approach to this problem would be to leave the investment portfolio to your children in a trust created by your will. Under the terms of the trust, the income would be distributed to your spouse only if the trustee determines a specified financial hardship exists. After your spouse's death, the trust assets would be distributed to your children in accordance with the terms you establish for the trust.

Finally, if you and your spouse have a combined net worth over $1.2 million, consider combining the marital deduction with annual gifts to minimize your estate taxes. If these two techniques together won't eliminate your estate tax bite, you should discuss with your estate planner what other options may be available to you. One approach he or she might suggest is the tax-smart use of charitable giving.

Charities in Estate Planning

The use of charitable giving can be an important part of every estate plan; for certain high net worth people, however, it is an option which must be given serious consideration. Beyond the obvious altruistic and societal benefits of charitable giving, certain provisions of the tax law make such giving an attractive option.

First, any amounts you leave to a qualified charity are not included in your net worth for estate tax purposes. Thus, outright charitable gifts sometimes can solve your estate tax problems.

> **Example:** Again consider the couple from the beginning of this section whose combined net worth, $615,000, was just over the exemption limit. If this couple left, say, $25,000 to charity in their wills, they would avoid Federal estate taxes altogether.

If your net worth is high enough that you can't afford or don't want to make the large outright gifts necessary to come down under $600,000, there is a family of charitable trusts which may solve your problems. Charitable trusts are complex mechanisms that should only be established with the assistance of a competent professional, but, in the right circumstances, they can be a perfect way to beat the estate tax rap. There are three kinds of charitable trusts: the charitable lead trust, the charitable unitrust, and the charitable remainder trust. Of these, the charitable remainder trust (CRT) seems to be the most popular estate planning tool in this area.

The mechanics of the CRT are fairly straight-forward. You place money or other property into a trust; the trust pays you income for a specified period of time, and then gives the remainder to the charity you designated when creating the trust. The assets you placed in the trust are no longer yours, so they're not counted in computing your net worth. You've lowered your estate tax bite correspondingly.

Part of what makes CRTs so appealing is their income tax treatment: they give rise to an immediate charitable deduction. The amount of the deduction is based on the present value of the trust assets to be distributed to the charity, and is determined based on IRS tables. Your total charitable deductions, including the deduction generated by a CRT, cannot exceed 50% of your income for any year (the percentage can be even lower when property other than cash is donated); however, any unused amounts can be carried forward and applied to offset future income for up to 5 years.

In the less popular charitable lead trust, the mechanics are merely reversed; the income interest is given to a qualifying charity for a specified number of years, and the remainder passes to the beneficiaries you designate in the trust agreement (e.g., your children).

Remember, charitable giving is an important part of estate planning, but it is not a panacea; you still end up giving away a chunk of your net worth to charity, so make sure you're motivated at least in part by charitable purposes. Don't be fooled into thinking charitable trusts always result in a wash (although, in the right circumstances, they do). Nevertheless, most people want to include charitable giving in their estate plans, and charitable trusts can make such generosity pay off!

Paying the Estate Tax Bill

What happens if you just can't avoid having your estate pay taxes? In most cases, the government expects its money within 9 months of your death. There are, however, steps you can take to assure that your estate is liquid at that critical and difficult time.

First, if your estate consists largely of a small business or family farm, the tax law includes an extended payment plan of sorts, which lets you stretch out the estate tax bill over a 14 year period. The rules for qualifying for this option are complex, so check with your estate planner to see if extended payments will be available to your estate.

If you don't qualify for extended payments (or even if you do), there may be another way to help fund your estate tax liability: survivorship life insurance. Also called "second-to-die" insurance, these policies insure two lives, and as the name suggests, they don't pay any benefit until the second insured dies. Such insurance is usually purchased by a husband and wife, and the estate of the second spouse to die is the beneficiary. In essence, purchasing such insurance allows you to "pre-pay" your estate tax liability through the insurance company -- often for pennies on the dollar.

> **Example:** A couple in their mid-sixties anticipates an estate tax liability of $290,000. They purchase a $500,000 survivorship policy for seven $10,000 annual premiums. They've purchased $500,000 in estate tax payments for $70,000.

In this example, the couple's estate tax liability was only $290,000, yet they purchased $500,000 in insurance. Why? Because, as with all other forms of insurance, the proceeds from a "second-to-die" policy are included in the net worth of the second spouse. Estate tax must be paid on those proceeds, so the total amount insured has to be "grossed up" to account for this. Your estate planner or insurance representative should be able to help you gross up your figures accordingly.

> **Example:** In the last example, based on the couple's estate tax bracket, the additional $500,000 in net worth added another $210,000 to their estate tax bill. This additional amount had to be funded with insurance. Even with this additional tax, the insurance is still a good deal; the couple in this example funded their Federal estate tax obligation for about 24 cents on the dollar ($70,000 total premiums/ $290,000 original estate tax liability = 24 cents)!

To save even more money, ask your estate planner about setting up a trust to hold and pay for the survivorship insurance. If the trust is structured properly, the proceeds won't be included in the net worth of the second spouse to die.

As with any insurance purchase, shop around carefully when buying a survivorship policy. Be skeptical when reviewing insurance company policy illustrations; not surprisingly, they try to put a good spin on things. They seldom forecast a worst case scenario (for example, what happens to premium prices if one spouse dies shortly after the policy's inception), and the illustrations are rarely if ever guaranteed. Make sure you're working with a broker or agent you trust and that he or she is representing a highly-rated insurance company. Make sure you've gotten all the facts up front. And, make sure you're getting the best possible value for your insurance dollar.

TAX SMART INVESTMENTS

The tax law is making it harder and harder to shelter your hard-earned income from taxes -- the first time around. However, there are ways to invest your after-tax dollars to be certain that the income they earn takes maximum advantage of the remaining incentives ("loop-holes" if you're a cynic!) in the law. This section explores several of the more time-tested approaches to tax-smart investing.

Remember that none of these investments alone is the answer to all your troubles. In fact, some of these investments may be down right inappropriate for your financial situation or risk tolerance. Direct ownership of real estate, for example, is not for new investors or for those with only a small amount to risk. Seek competent professional advice in constructing a balance and diversified portfolio that fits your individual needs.

Municipal Bonds

Municipal bonds are probably the most popular form of tax-advantaged investing. That's because, under almost all circumstances, income generated by the bonds is exempt from Federal income tax. On top of that, in most states, if you purchase in-state municipal bonds, they're free of state and local taxes as well. For people who derive a substantial percentage of their income from interest on their assets, this can mean huge tax savings.

> **Example:** You have $10,000 to invest. As a conservative investor, you want to avoid as much as possible any risk to your principal. You could invest your funds in a corporate bond earning 8% or a municipal bond paying 6.5%. While the corporate bond sounds like a better deal at first blush, a closer look at the after-tax numbers shows this isn't so. The municipal bond will pay you $650 in interest, but, assuming its been issued by the state in which you reside, it's completely tax free. With regard to the corporate bond, in the 15% bracket, you would pay $120 in Federal income tax on your $800 interest income, leaving you with a return of $680 before state income taxes. If you live in a state with

at least a 4% income tax rate (and many are higher), the bond is a better deal ($800 x 4% = $32; $680 - $32 = $648).

The situation is even more compelling in the 28% bracket. The municipal bond still earns you $650, but the corporate bond now costs you $224 in Federal income tax ($800 x 28% = $224), leaving you with a return of $576 before state income taxes ($800 - $224 = $576). In the 31% bracket, the difference becomes substantial. The Federal income tax on the corporate bond rises to $248 ($800 x 31% = $248), and the net return shrinks to $552 ($800- $248 = $552). The municipal bond leaves you with about $100 more in your pocket -- and that's before state and local taxes!!!

As you can see, the higher your tax bracket, the more valuable municipal bonds are to you. That's why they were recommended earlier in this book for investors affected by the new 36% and 39.6% tax brackets. The return is probably better on municipal bonds than the after-tax return on taxable investments.

There are, of course, investment risks inherent in buying municipal bonds. It doesn't happen often, but the issuer can default. This risk can be minimized by purchasing only high-grade single issues, AA or above. Even better, consider a municipal bond fund. Like stock mutual funds, these entities invest in a variety of bond issues, thereby spreading the risk over a large number of holdings. A bond fund will also make you slightly less vulnerable to the risk that a significant change in interest rates will decrease the value of investments.

There's a good quality municipal bond investment for just about every state. Even if you can't find a municipal bond issued by your state or a bond fund restricted to investing in your state, municipal bonds still are a good deal. They're free of Federal income tax regardless of which state you invest in. It's the state income tax savings that give in-state bonds an added appeal. Municipal bonds should be a part of every serious investor's portfolio.

Real Estate

Investing directly in real estate can be one of the best ways to generate tax losses. It can also be one of the riskiest. It provides one of the few remaining opportunities where excess losses can be used to offset other sources of income to reduce taxes. At the same time, the difficulties of owning real estate -- finding tenants, collecting rent, evicting tenants, making repairs, market fluctuations, and potential illiquidity -- suggest it's not for the squeamish. Here, then, are the rules, the risks, and the rewards of direct investment in real estate.

The tax law allows you to deduct up $25,000 in excess rental real estate losses (i.e., losses in excess of your rental income) if you meet several rules. First, you must own the real estate directly (e.g., you cannot own it through a limited partnership; if you are a partner in a general partnership, however, you qualify). Next, if you own the property jointly with others, your ownership interest must be greater than 10%. Additionally, you must "actively participate" in the management of the property (more on this later). Finally, the amount of your deduction gets phased out as your income rises. If your income is under $100,000 you can deduct up to the full $25,000. Above $100,000, the $25,000 limit gets reduced until it reaches zero at $150,000 in income. Thus, this technique is not available to you for any year in which your income exceeds $150,000.

If your income consistently exceeds $150,000, you should consider investing in rental real estate purely from the perspective of its potential appreciation. Under current law, it can't offer you any special tax write-offs. If you're a high income-earner who has been bitten by the real estate bug, a vacation home may be a better bet for you than rental real estate. Although it can't generate the tax losses that rental property can, a vacation home still allows you to deduct mortgage interest and property taxes. Again, though, in order for such an investment to make financial sense, you should have some indication that the property will appreciate sufficiently to make up for its negative cash flow -- or you better enjoy the place a lot!

A quick word about "active participation": IRS actually

interprets this requirement fairly broadly. You can still employ a management company or rental agent to assist you in running your real estate activities. You don't have to hammer the nails or screw the screws yourself. You do have to be a part of management decisions, however, like selecting tenants or setting rents. When it's time for capital improvements, you should be the one calling the shots. You also should keep good records to prove that you participated in the management of your rental real estate.

The rewards of qualifying for this deduction have already briefly been touched upon: deducting excess losses against other sources of income, such as wages, interest, dividends or business income.

> **Example:** You own a condo that you rent for $500 per month ($6,000 per year). However, after you pay the mortgage, condo fees, property taxes, and claim depreciation, the property costs you $7,000 per year. Assuming your income is under $100,000, the $1,000 loss ($6,000 - $7,000 = $1,000) can be used to offset your wages, interest, or dividends. If you are in the 15% bracket, this will reduce your Federal taxes by $150, and $280 if you are in the 28% bracket.

Clearly, these rules can make rental real estate a singularly attractive investment from a tax perspective. However, how you generate these "excess losses" without also having to spend a lot of money "out of pocket" can be tricky, and it highlights the first of many risks involved in direct investment in real estate.

It is not always easy to find a real estate investment that will generate tax losses without also generating real economic losses to the investor, but it can be done. The key is to consider the value of the depreciation deduction in determining whether a loss is a real loss or just a tax loss. The tax law allows you to recover the cost of your real estate investment over its "useful life". The tax law specifies what the useful life for real estate is -- 27.5 years for residential, 39 years otherwise. So, each year you can deduct about 3.6% of the cost of your investment real estate.

> **Example:** Consider the example above. Suppose that, out of your $7,000 in expenses, $4,500 was for mortgage interest, $1,000 was for condo fees, and $1,500 was for depreciation. Since that $1,500 didn't really come out of your pocket (at least not the same way the mortgage interest and condo fees did), it is not a cash flow loss. It is, however, a tax deduction. Moreover, since you only spent $5,500 out-of-pocket" ($4,500 + $1,000 = $5,500), you've earned $500 more in rent than you've laid out in expenses that year. The net result: a $1,000 deduction for excess losses, and $500 in "tax-free" income!

Sounds too good to be true? That's because sometimes it can be. In the example above, what would happen if the condo sat vacant for one month? Or two? What if your tenant didn't pay rent for a month, or if major repairs were required? Expenses associated with real estate are not always as predictable as with other investments, and cash flow can vary from year to year. Some landlords find themselves in a situation where the property is generating not only tax losses, but real out-of-pocket economic losses as well.

Small economic losses aren't always a sign that you've made a bad investment. If the property appreciates by more than the amount of the loss, it is possible to still come out ahead. But, situations like these quickly become speculative, and are best left to investors who can afford to lose the money involved. Although appreciation may help you through a dry patch, it's not always a guarantee anymore.

Appreciation -- or the lack thereof -- suggests another source of risk for investing in real estate. As has been noted elsewhere, real estate values these days can be very fluid, and today's solid investment can be tomorrow's albatross. Unless you are very familiar with real estate trends in the area where you plan to invest, don't make appreciation a major factor in your decision-making process.

The last source of risk in real estate investments is illiquidity.

Put simply, this means you might not be able to sell (liquidate) your real estate investment when you want to (or need to). The real estate market is a textbook example of the forces of supply and demand, and sometimes houses just don't sell at any price. Real estate should not be viewed as a short-term investment by most investors; if you take the plunge, prepare to be in for the long haul.

While all these risks sound pretty scary (and with good reason), real estate can be an important part of your investment portfolio, and, if you qualify, a wonderful tax-advantaged asset. Moreover, there are steps you can take to minimize the risks, both before and after you buy.

First, spend a lot of time "going over the numbers" before you buy. Hire a number-cruncher if you have to; a good one is worth his or her weight in gold. They can help you determine whether your cash flow is going to be negative just on your tax return, or also in your bank account. They should also be able to tell you whether the deal you propose makes economic sense, or whether it would be more profitable to just park your money in a mutual fund. Next, be slow and deliberate when selecting a property; don't let anyone pressure you into buying before you've done a thorough analysis. In the current market, there's no deal so good that it can't wait until you're good and ready. Consider the pros and cons of residential versus commercial property. Commercial property can have a higher vacancy rate, but being a residential landlord can cause lots of headaches. Also, screen your tenants carefully; bad tenants are guaranteed to be your single biggest source of trouble. References and credit reports are a must, along with as much in security deposits and rental deposits as your local law allows. Finally, make sure your budget for the investment sets aside a little each month to cover unforeseen contingencies -- repairs, late rent, and vacancies should all be planned for.

One last thing to consider about investing in rental real estate. Lest you be fooled into thinking the government is giving money away, you should know that all the depreciation you've been claiming while you own your property gets added to your gain when you sell it. This will add to your tax bill if your property has appreciated in value.

A final reminder: remember that these rules only apply to investment property, and not to your residence or a vacation home. Many of the things you can deduct for investment purposes (e.g., depreciation, condo fees, repairs) are not deductible when spent on your primary or secondary home.

Annuities

Annuities allow you to save money on a tax-advantaged basis. When you purchase an annuity, the income it earns is not taxed to you until you take it out. This, of course, usually happens in the form of a periodic payment at some future date. Annuities therefore are also a good retirement planning vehicle.

There are many different types of annuities. They are classified based on how they are purchased (single premium vs. periodic premiums), how they earn income (fixed rates or variable (i.e., market) rates), when they begin paying benefits (immediate vs. deferred), and to whom those benefits are paid (individual vs. joint).

The type of annuity appropriate for you depends on your age, the reason for purchasing the annuity, and your overall financial circumstances. Consult a tax advisor or financial planner before deciding what to purchase. There are a few things you should keep in mind, however, as you go through the process, remembering that annuities have been recommended here because they offer a form of tax-advantaged savings and investing.

First, unless you intend to begin drawing upon you annuity right away, you probably do not want to purchase a single premium annuity. As an investment vehicle, annuities that require monthly or quarterly premiums are the better way to help the average investor save as he or she goes.

Next, a fixed rate annuity works like a CD; it pays a fixed rate.

If your investment goals are more aggressive, a variable annuity allows you to participate in the greater rewards (and higher risks) of an investment similar to mutual funds. Variable annuities therefore can be a good tax-advantaged surrogate for mutual fund investing. In both cases, however, you enjoy the advantage of deferring tax on your investment's income until it is paid out to you.

Third, since the goal here is investing, you want a deferred annuity, and not one that's immediately payable. The longer your money stays out of your hands, the longer part of it stays out of the government's.

As always, review critically the information concerning expected return on investment presented to you by the company offering the annuity; not surprisingly, it's trying to put the best foot forward.

Oil & Gas

The tax law has many special rules for oil and gas drilling activities. Because the development of domestic energy sources is important for the country, many of those provisions are favorable to investors in oil or gas drilling activities. Two particular aspects of oil and gas investments provide a tax benefit.

First, the deduction for something called "intangible drilling costs" will generate an immediate tax loss in the first year or two of your investment. You can use this loss to offset other sources of income and lower your overall tax bill. Second, an annual allowance for something called "percentage depletion" will offset some of the income the venture produces in its later years.

In order to qualify for these benefits, you must participate directly in the drilling venture. This means you cannot be a limited partner. This involves a greater degree of risk, so make sure any venture you consider investing in is heavily insured.

As always, make sure your investment makes good economic sense before you sign up, or it can't possibly make good tax sense. It also must be consistent with your financial goals, appropriate for your risk tolerance, and in line with your overall financial situation.

Low Income Housing

In order to encourage investment in low income housing projects, the tax law provides a credit to the property's owners. Complying with all of the applicable rules is quite complex, and a state or local housing agency is usually involved in the process. OBRA 93 made the low income housing credit permanent (it had expired), and it is discussed in the Chapter of this book regarding tax law changes affecting real estate.

Basically, if you invest in a project that qualifies for the credit, you realize an immediate tax benefit because of it. You also can receive rental income from the property and enjoy appreciation on it. Don't be misled, these are legitimate housing projects for low to moderate income workers and seniors, not welfare deals. Your financial or investment advisor can probably direct you to an appropriate low-income housing investment in your area.

Historic Rehabilitation

If you rehabilitate property built before 1936, you can claim a tax credit equal to 10% of your qualified expenditures (20% if the property's certified historic). A complicated formula limits the amount of credit you can claim in any one year; unused credits can be carried forward to future years, so the benefit can still be substantial. A credit is a direct dollar-for-dollar offset against your tax bill, so the right "rehab" project can be a great tax deal. As always, your investment must make good financial sense. If the income or appreciation you anticipate on the finished product doesn't justify the initial investment expenditures, the project probably isn't worth undertaking. The tax credit, however, can help push marginal projects into the black. If you're considering purchasing a "fixer-upper" in order to enjoy the extra appreciation in value that renovations sometimes offer, look into purchasing property that qualifies for the credit. It can make your efforts even more valuable.

ENGAGING IN BRACKET "ARBITRAGE"

"Arbitrage" is a fancy word that relates to timing one's transactions in order to maximize their return. In the stock market, arbitrage might mean buying securities on one exchange where they're trading for a lower price while simultaneously selling the same securities on another exchange where they're trading at a higher price. With the advent of computers, this sort of basic arbitrage opportunity rarely arises anymore, but there are individuals who make very handsome incomes by engaging in more sophisticated forms of market arbitrage.

Tax bracket "arbitrage" involves a similar shifting on the taxpayer's part. Bracket arbitrage involves legally moving income from a higher bracket to a lower bracket. There are two ways you can engage in tax bracket arbitrage: shift income to a lower-bracket taxpayer (usually a family member), or shift it to a lower-bracket year of your own.

Shifting income to a lower-bracket taxpayer is often a straightforward affair: simply transfer title to the assets producing the income to a relative or friend in a lower tax bracket. Of course, once you transfer title to an asset, you no longer have control over it. Not surprisingly, therefore, most people are very selective with regard to whom they transfer their assets. A spouse, who normally would be the logical choice for such a transfer, will not be of much help in this instance. He or she is already filing joint returns with you, which means you haven't successfully shifted income out of your bracket by moving it from your name to your spouse's.

Children are the next logical choice for transferring assets. Someday it probably would be theirs, anyway. However, the effectiveness of shifting income to one's children is limited by a part of the law known as the "Kiddie Tax". The Kiddie Tax was created as part of the Tax Reform Act of 1986. Congress perceived that many parents were using their children to shift income and pay tax at lower rates. So the restrictions, which apply to the "unearned" income of children under age 14, work as follows: a child's first $600 in income is tax free, the next $600 is taxed at 15%, and the remainder is taxed at his or her parent's marginal rate.

> **Example:** Your daughter, age 12, earns $1,500 in taxable interest income each year. The first $600 of that income is tax free to her. The next $600 is taxed at 15%, or $90. The last $300 will be taxed at your marginal rate -- $84 if you're in the 28% bracket, for a total tax of $174.

Of course, this $174 compares favorably to the $420 in income tax you'd pay on the interest if the account were in your name ($1,500 x 28% = $420, assuming you're in the 28% bracket), so there is still some potential for tax bracket arbitrage by titling some of your accounts in your children's names. The Kiddie Tax rules don't eliminate this tax savings strategy, but they do limit its utility considerably.

The Kiddie Tax rules don't apply to a child's earned income (e.g., wages from part-time jobs, etc.), and they don't apply once a child reaches age 14. Parents can elect to report and pay Kiddie Tax on their returns, or they file separate returns for their children.

Other relatives also can be good "partners" for tax bracket arbitrage, but there must be some motivation other than tax avoidance or IRS may re-characterize the transaction as a sham if it is audited. Elderly parents often can fill this bill.

> **Example:** Your mother is a widow in her late 60's. She is in the 15% tax bracket, and you are in the 31% bracket. Although you do not claim her as a dependent, you do provide your mother with about $2,000 in financial assistance annually. If you and your spouse transfer into your mother's name a brokerage account valued at $20,000 and returning about 11% (or $2,200) annually, she will still receive about the same amount of money from you after she pays taxes. You, however, will have reduced a $682 tax bill ($2,200 x 31% = $682) to $330 ($2,200 x 15% = $330).

You should also remember the Gift Tax rules (discussed earlier under the estate planning section) when shifting income-producing assets. Once you give more than $10,000 ($20,000 for you and your spouse) per year to any one recipient, you have created a taxable gift. Make sure that your arbitrage activities don't collide with the Gift Tax rules.

The other form of tax bracket arbitrage involves timing your items of income or deduction in order to ensure that they provide the maximum tax benefit to you. In general, where you have the ability to control the timing, you should try to recognize income in a year where you expect to be taxed in a lower bracket and pay deductible expenses in a year in which you will be taxed at a higher bracket. Thus, you compare your tax bracket for two years in order to determine which year is more advantageous for you. Usually opportunities for this kind of tax planning occur toward the end of the calendar year.

> **Example 1:** In December of 19X1, you decide to sell some of your stock for a $10,000 gain. You expect to be in the 28% tax bracket that year, which means you will pay $2,800 in income tax on the gain. However, you also expect to be in the 15% bracket in 19X2, which means you would pay only $1,500 in tax on the gain. By waiting until January to sell your stock, you could save $1,300 in taxes ($2,800 - $1,500 = $1,300).

> **Example 2:** Your property tax bill ($2,500) is due in February of 19X2. However, you will be retiring in that year, and expect that your tax bracket will go down from 28% in 19X1 to 15% in 19X2. If you pay the bill in December of 19X1, you will generate an extra $325 in tax savings for yourself, assuming you itemize your deductions in both 19X1 and 19X2 (($2,500 x 28%) - ($2,500 x 15%) = $325).

Also, remember that this form of bracket arbitrage can work both ways, depending on which way your tax bracket is heading from year to year.

Example: Your property tax bill ($2,500) is due in January of each year, so you usually pay it in December. However, you know that you will be receiving a promotion in the first quarter of 19X2, which will move you from the 15% to the 28% tax bracket. By waiting until January to pay your taxes this year, you will generate an extra $325 in tax savings in 19X2.

The hard part about this kind of tax bracket arbitrage is figuring out what tax bracket you're going to be in for each of the two years you are comparing. You need to have a good sense of your finances for two years in order to be successful at it. If you have steady income and expenses and feel confident about your projections, a few hours with a calculator one weekend in December could be advantageous. On the other hand, if your income and expenses fluctuate, this tax strategy may not be for you.

There also are some important legal limits on your ability to play tax bracket arbitrage this way, and it is critical that you understand them before trying it. First, these rules only apply to "cash basis" taxpayers. Virtually all individuals and most sole proprietors report their income and expenses on what IRS calls the "cash basis". This means that they pay taxes on the income in the year it is actually earned, and deduct their expenses in the year actually paid. (Many businesses, by contrast, are "accrual basis" taxpayers. This more complicated method requires that income be recognized or expenses be deducted in the year they are accrued by the taxpayer, regardless of the date of actual payment.) Unless you filed some very complicated paperwork with the IRS, you are probably a cash basis taxpayer.

This discussion also assumes your tax year ends on December 31st, because virtually all individual's tax years end then. Again, unless you filed some complicated forms with IRS at a very tender age, you are probably on a calendar tax year. If by chance you're not, however, simply substitute the last month of your tax year for "December" in this section to understand how this technique applies to you.

Next, with regard to the timing of income, it is important to understand that, once you have control of the money, you no longer have the ability to defer taxation of it until the next year. This concept is called "constructive receipt" in tax jargon. Once you have constructive receipt of income, you must pay tax on it.

> **Example:** You received a $3,000 check from a brokerage account on December 29th. You know you will be in a lower tax bracket the following year, so you wait until January 2nd to deposit the check. The tax law deems you to be in constructive receipt of the income on December 29th and you must pay tax on it in the earlier year and in the higher bracket.

If you are a salaried employee, you have constructive receipt of your wages once you are entitled to receive them, so you can't ask your employer to hold your last paycheck of the year until January. (They probably wouldn't do it, anyway!)

Also, with regard to the timing of deductions, while pre-paying certain expenses (e.g., property taxes, charitable contributions) in December can help generate some extra deductions for the current year, there is a limit to IRS' tolerance of this practice. As mentioned earlier in this book, the general rule of thumb is that you should not try to pre-pay deductible expenses more than one year in advance, absent compelling or unusual circumstances.

Finally, tax bracket arbitrage with respect to deferring the payment of deductible expenses only makes sense if there is a big jump in rates. For example, if you can shift a deduction from a 15% rate in 19X1 to a 28% rate in 19X2, it is a good idea to wait to January to pay the expense. However, if the shift is only from the 28% bracket in 19X1 to the 31% bracket in 19X2, it probably makes more economic sense to take advantage of the deduction in the earlier year. The small (i.e., 3%) tax advantage in the later year is more than offset by the time value of the money saved by lowering your taxes in the earlier year.

ENGAGING IN DEDUCTION "ARBITRAGE"

If you're a taxpayer whose deductions routinely put you on the border between itemizing and claiming the standard deduction, you may be able to benefit from "deduction arbitrage". Like rate arbitrage, this form of tax planning requires you to time the payment of your deductions in order to maximize their (tax) effectiveness for you. However, instead of accelerating or deferring expenses in order to take advantage of a rate differential from year to year, you're going to "batch" your deductions in order to take advantage of the value of the standard deduction.

This strategy isn't for everyone. It's really only for people whose deductions hover right around the standard deduction threshold each year. If you're always above that amount, or always below it, you probably can't profit from this technique. Thus, for example, if you own a home and pay mortgage interest each year, you probably have too many itemized deductions to profit from deduction arbitrage.

For 1993, the standard deductions are as follows:

Single	$3,700
Married Filing Joint	$6,200
Married Filing Separate	$3,100
Head of Household	$5,450

If your deductions are on the border, consider this example of how the technique works:

Example: You are a single taxpayer with a salary of $35,000, putting you in the 28% bracket. You have $2,000 withheld annually in state income tax, make annual charitable contributions of $2,000, and pay $300 annually (in two semi-annual installments) in personal property tax on your automobile. Your total deductions are $4,300, and you qualify to itemize. However, you are only $600 over the 1993 standard deduction amount ($4,300 - $3,700 = $600), so these deductions are only worth $168 more in additional tax savings than the government was going to give you anyway ($600 x 28% = $168).

There is a way to restructure your deductions, however, in order to save more. Try paying them this way:

EXPENSE	YEAR 1	YEAR 2
State Tax	$2,000	$2,000
Contributions	$3,000	$1,000
Personal Property Tax	$ 450	$ 150
TOTAL DEDUCTIONS:	$5,450	$3,150

This payment pattern recognizes the following non-tax realities: you cannot control the timing of your state tax withholding, you probably would not forego charitable contributions altogether every other year, and you can only partially pre-pay your personal property taxes. However, if you maintain this alternating pattern over time, you will save $154 over every two year cycle.

Here's how that figure is computed: Assume Year 1 is 1993. The value of your itemized deductions increased from $168 to $490 ($5450 - $3,700 = $1,750; $1,750 x 28% = $490). That's an additional Year 1 savings of $322. Meanwhile, in Year 2 (1994), you've lost that extra $168, because in that year deductions -- $3,150 -- won't be enough to itemize. This leaves a net savings of $154 ($322 - $168 = $154).

The payment pattern will vary depending on personal circumstances, so your actual tax savings will be different. moreover, it is not always going to be possible to control the timing of all your deductions. However, if you're on the itemizing border, it's likely this strategy can pay off for you.

Remember, as with bracket arbitrage, you can only pre-pay expenses so far in advance before the IRS takes an interest in your tax planning. In the example above, you only pre-paid personal property taxes six months out. Also remember that the standard deduction is indexed for inflation every year, so you need to be sharp with figures in order to use this strategy. If you are, it's a nice way to shave a couple hundred dollars off your tax bill.

There's one other downside to beware of with this technique: state income taxes. If you're in a state that requires you to itemize deductions on its return when you itemized on the Federal (and vice versa if you don't), this strategy may leave you paying more in state taxes than you save in Federal taxes. Whether this will happen in your case depends on three things: (1) how big your state's standard deduction is; (2) if your state requires you to handle your deductions the same way you do on your Federal returns (i.e., if you itemize on the Federal, you must itemize on the state; and, (3) how much of your itemized deductions consist of state income tax withholdings. Because these factors vary widely from state to state and taxpayer to taxpayer, it's hard to generalize. But if you live in a state with a high tax rate, do the math for both Federal and state returns before you engage in deduction arbitrage.

USE AND MISUSE OF EE BONDS

EE U.S. Government Savings Bonds offer smart investors a couple of tax-saving opportunities. They also offer at least one seeming opportunity that can actually turn out to be a tax trap for the unwary. EE Bonds offer these planning opportunities because they give you the option of either paying tax on interest income as it is earned or deferring the tax until the bond matures. There's a general rule in tax planning that there is value in deferring taxes whenever possible. Applied to EE Bonds, this rule would mean that you generally would benefit by electing to defer recognition of the interest income on a bond until it matures. However, there can be some situations, particularly when the bond is titled in a child's name, where the Kiddie Tax rules (discussed in the section on tax bracket arbitrage) make it advantageous for you to recognize the interest income in the year it is earned.

> **Example:** Your 7-year old son owns $7,000 in EE Bonds. He earns $400 in interest on them annually. If they are his only source of income, he would pay no tax on the $400 he earns each year. However, if he defers recognition of the interest income until the bonds mature, he very likely would be required to pay tax on at least some of the income. Assume for example, he was given the bonds at birth and owns them until age 20. That would give him $8,000 in deferred interest income ($400 x 20 = $8,000), some of which almost certainly would be taxable -- how much would depend on his other sources of income at the time.

As long as the amount of interest income is beneath the Kiddie Tax limits, you (or, technically, your child) probably are better off recognizing it in the year it is earned than deferring it. This is certainly the case if the interest income falls below the $600 limit, and may also be the case even for the $1,200 limit. In essence, you are using the lower Kiddie Tax brackets to your advantage. In the process, you are turning what was supposed to be a tax penalty into a tax advantage. Just remember that, above $1,200 in interest income, this benefit is lost and the additional amount is taxed at your marginal rate.

One good use of EE Bonds is for financing a child's college education. Under certain circumstances, not only can the interest earned on EE bonds be deferred for tax purposes, but, it can be eliminated altogether when the bonds are redeemed. In order to qualify for excluding EE Bond interest from your taxable income, you must meet the following restrictions. (1) The bonds must be issued after 1989. (2) You must be at least age 24 when you purchase the bond, and the bond must be registered solely in your name (it can be registered jointly with a spouse). This effectively means the bonds probably will have to be titled in your name, not your child's. (3) The bonds won't qualify for the exclusion if they are transferred to you by someone else. (4) They also won't qualify if you transfer them to the educational institution; you must redeem them. (5) The expenses must be paid by you for yourself, your spouse, or your dependent child. (6) Eligible expenses include only tuition and fees (i.e., not room, board, club, or sports dues). (7) If the total amount you redeem exceeds your eligible expenses, you must include a portion of the excess in income for the year you redeem the bonds. (8) This tax break phases out once your income exceeds $68,250 for joint returns and $45,500 for single filers (adjusted annually for inflation).

Although these rules may seem like a lot of trouble, the tax advantage can be significant. Excluding 15 or 20 years of accumulated interest from income can be a tremendous help in meeting the high cost of a college education. EE Bonds should be a part of most parents' savings program for their younger children's college expenses.

One final word of advice: make sure savings bonds are a good economic investment before buying them. As of this writing, EE Bonds are only paying 4% interest, and that may make them an inferior investment for you, even with their tax advantages. Always remember that your decisions have to make good financial sense, and not just good tax sense.

SAVVY RETIREMENT PLAN WITHDRAWALS

If you have been participating in some form of tax-deferred retirement plan -- an IRA, SEP, 401(k), Keogh, or employer plan, you eventually will have to make withdrawals from your plan. If the funds were not taxed going into your plan, they are going to be taxed coming out. The key is for you to learn the ways to minimize the tax bite on your retirement plan withdrawals.

The types of strategies available to you to minimize taxes on retirement plan withdrawals vary based on your age, how long you've bene participating in the plan, how much you're taking out, and what type of plan it is. The following general discussion should help you determine which approach will save you the most money. However, if you're still not confident about what to do with your retirement savings, hire a number-cruncher. You have tens, or perhaps hundreds, of thousands of dollars in your plan, so the stakes are too high to risk a mistake. As with estate planning, a good retirement planner will more than earn his or her fee in the amount of taxes they'll save you.

As a general proposition, you are well-advised to keep money in your retirement plans for as long as possible. As was discussed above (in the section on retirement savings), your retirement accounts grow without paying tax until they're withdrawn. This means that interest, dividends, and capital gains earned by your retirement assets can grow for years and years free of income tax. However, there are a few -- relatively rare -- situations in which you need to withdraw funds from your plan or plans before you otherwise might. Read the next section (on retirement plan traps) to find out about how this can affect you.

Some employer plans, particularly 401(k)s, allow participants to take loans against their cash balances. If you need money and this option is available to you, use it instead of making a withdrawal. Essentially, you're making a loan to yourself, and the interest you pay on the funds you borrow gets credited back to your account! Loans are not available for IRAs and SEPs.

Premature Distribution Penalties

In any event, it's a good idea to wait until you're at least age 59-1/2 before withdrawing any retirement funds. If you take anything out before then, you're subject to a 10% penalty tax in addition to any income tax you owe.

> **Example:** At age 40, you withdraw $10,000 from your IRA account to purchase a new car. You are in the 28% bracket. When you file your next tax return, you will pay $2,800 in Federal income tax ($10,000 x 28% = $2,800), plus $1,000 in penalty tax ($10,000 x 10% = $1,000). This leaves you with a net of $6,200 on this transaction before you pay any applicable state income taxes ($10,000 - $2,800 - $1,000 = $6,200).

Clearly, the approach in the example above was not a good way to purchase your new car. You've only realized about 60 cents on the dollar from the amount you've withdrawn.

The 10% penalty tax also will be applied to most distributions you receive from an employer's plan before age 59-1/2, if you decide to keep them. These distributions usually occur either when you leave your job or when your employer terminates its plan. Tax-smart ways of handling these distributions and avoiding the penalty tax on them are discussed below.

There are some exceptions to the 10% penalty tax. If you die before age 59-1/2, your beneficiaries won't be required to pay the tax when they withdraw your retirement plan proceeds. Similarly, if you are disabled before 59-1/2, you can withdraw from retirement accounts free of the 10% penalty. Of course, in both situations, the regular income tax due on the withdrawal still must be paid.

Annuitized Distributions

There is one other way to take money out of your retirement plans before 59-1/2 without incurring the 10% penalty, but it's only a practical solution in a small number of cases. The tax law allows you to avoid the penalty if you make a "series of substantially equal periodic payments" from your account. This means that, if you annuitize your account balance and make equal withdrawals over your life expectancy, your withdrawals will be free of the penalty tax.

For all practical purposes, this annuity option only works with IRAs or SEPs. Employer plans usually do not give you the option of making withdrawals before you retire or leave employment (401(k)s can be an exception to this). Moreover, when you're ready to retire, you don't have to worry about the penalty tax (you're over 59-1/2), and you can take an annuity directly from your employer's plan. Remember, however, that your IRAs can be funded from a variety of sources: your pre-tax contributions, your post-tax contributions, and rollovers of distributions from an employer's plan. (Again, rollover distributions are discussed below.) For simplicity's sake, it will be assumed in this discussion that your IRAs are funded exclusively with pre-tax contributions (i.e., all of your contributions were deducted on previous tax returns). If you made any non-deductible contributions to your IRA accounts, the pro-rata share of distributions attributable to those contributions (but not any earnings on them) is free of tax.

While this "annuity exception" to the penalty rule may seem like a golden opportunity, it has two very serious practical drawbacks. First, you must make withdrawals at least every year until you reach 59-1/2. Second, you must have a very large account balance to make this technique worthwhile.

> **Example 1:** You are 45 years old with a $10,000 IRA account balance. Your life expectancy is 85 years, or 40 more years. In order to withdraw the funds from your IRA without being subject to the 10% penalty, you would have to withdraw $250 from your account each year until you reach age 59-1/2 ($10,000/40 = $250).

> **Example 2:** Change the circumstances in Example 1 somewhat. Assume your IRA account balance is $200,000. now you can withdraw $5,000 each year without paying the penalty tax ($200,000/40 = $5,000).

Clearly, the tiny amount of money you would realize in Example 1 isn't going to do you very much good. And, while you've avoided the penalty tax, you still have to pay regular income taxes on the $250. Annuitized distributions don't make a lot of sense for "small" account balances. Depending on your overall circumstances and the purposes for which you seek to withdraw the money, however, the approach in Example 2 may be beneficial for you. For example, depending on the availability of other assets, it may be helpful in meeting the cost of your children's college educations. Or, if it fits in with your overall financial and personal goals, perhaps it can help you pay off a mortgage in time for early retirement.

This technique is not for everyone; in fact its only going to work for the exceptional few. Not many people have high enough IRA balances to make this approach viable. Also, there's a downside to it that you must factor into your computations: it has the effect of drawing on your retirement savings about 10 to 20 years earlier than you probably were planning. You probably will need to adjust your retirement income expectations if you decide to use this approach. However, if you're one of the lucky few for whom it will work, it provides a nice way to supplement your current income or perhaps even expand your financial goals.

Rollover Distributions

So far, the discussion has focused on minimizing the impact of voluntary retirement plan withdrawals. What happens, however, when you receive a distribution involuntarily -- when you leave an employer or the employer terminates its plan? Sometimes nothing. Some employer plans, particularly defined benefit plans, don't always distribute your pension to you when you leave. Instead, they hold the funds and pay out only when you reach normal retirement age. Other times, if the plan is tied into an investment firm, that firm may let you keep your account with them even if you are no longer part of the plan. Occasionally, a new employer will allow you to transfer your savings directly from your old employer's plan into your new one. In each of these instances, you don't actually receive a distribution, so you don't have to worry about what to do with it.

Many times, however, this is not the case. A distribution from an employer's plan (or former employer's plan) often requires you to do a little planning and spend some time with paperwork in order to avoid big tax headaches. Congress has tightened the rules on rollovers considerably in recent years, making it even harder to protect your assets. Regardless of these new obstacles, the goal remains the same: you should try to roll your distribution over into another retirement account in order to avoid paying income tax on it -- and the 10% penalty tax if you're under 59-1/2.

First, the general rule: if you receive a lump-sum distribution from a retirement plan, you can avoid taxation on it by re-depositing the funds -- rolling them over -- into another retirement plan within 60 days. The rollover can be either into another employer's plan or into an IRA, but it must be done within 60 days to avoid tax; the time clock starts running the day the funds are disbursed to you. The rollover option is not available for periodic distributions from a retirement plan; i.e., once you retire and you start receiving your monthly pension check, you cannot roll it over to avoid paying taxes on it.

> **Example:** On 1 March, 19X1, you quit your job to start a new one. On 1 May, 19X1 your former employer notifies you that your pension plan account contains $10,000. On 1 June, 19X1 you open an IRA account with a local brokerage and authorize your former employer to deposit the funds in your new account. Your former employer does this on 15 June, 19X1. You have successfully rolled over your retirement plan balance without any adverse tax consequences.

Notice that in the example above you asked your employer to deposit the funds directly into your IRA account. That's because, if you had taken the distribution yourself, your employer would have been required to impose income tax withholding of 20% on the funds. This is so even if you intend to roll over 100% of the amount. Thus, n order to avoid adverse tax consequences, you would have to make up the other 20% of the distribution out of your own pocket, and then claim a credit for the withholding on the following year's tax return. If you didn't, that 20% your employer withheld wouldn't be considered rolled over, and you'd pay income and penalty taxes on it. Therefore, even though the money "washes out" after taxes, the impact on your cash flow makes direct distributions an unattractive option.

This withholding rule applies only to distributions from employer plans, and not to IRA distributions. If you think about it, withholding is a sensible requirement. What if you don't roll a distribution over? You're going to have a whopping tax bill the next April 15th, between the income tax and the penalty tax if you're under 59-1/2. The 20% withholding helps you meet your tax obligations. Besides, if you do a plan-to-plan or a plan-to-IRA transfer you avoid the withholding issue altogether. It's only when you take the distribution yourself and decide to roll it over yourself that things get difficult.

Example: On 1 March, 19X1, you quit your job to start a new one. On 1 May, 19X1 your former employer notifies you that your pension plan account contains $50,000. In order to avoid income tax and the 10% penalty, you decide to roll over the funds into an IRA account. You ask your employer to remit the funds to you for this purpose. The check arrives dated 15 May, 19X1 in the amount of $40,000 ($50,000 - 20% = $40,000). If you only deposit the $40,000 into an IRA, you will still owe income tax (and penalty tax if you are under 59-1/2) on the $10,000 your employer was required to withhold. In order to avoid this outcome, you will have to take the additional $10,000 from your own savings and deposit it into your new IRA by 14 July 19X1 (60 days after 15 May, 19X1). Of course, when you file your income taxes on 15 April, 19X2, you will be able to claim a $10,000 credit for the withheld taxes on your return.

As you can see, the out-of-pocket expense of rolling over retirement plan distributions yourself can be prohibitive. In order to avoid the pitfalls and vagaries of retirement distributions, then, you need to remember two simple rules: always roll over your lump-sum distributions to avoid income tax and the 10% penalty tax, and always do a direct plan-to-plan or plan-to-IRA rollover to avoid 20% tax withholding.

There's one other strategy involving the rollover rules you should be aware of. It can provide you with a short-term, interest-free loan if you use it properly. Remember, though, that the only type of retirement plan it works with is IRAs. In part,that's because lump-sum IRA distributions aren't subject to the 20% tax withholding rules described above.

If you withdraw funds from an IRA and redeposit them within 60 days, there are no tax consequences to the transaction. The purpose of this rule is to give you time to move your IRA assets from one investment to another. But, the law imposes no restrictions on what you can do with the money for the 60 days you have it. Thus, these funds can be a helpful source of short-term loans. This can be especially helpful for small businesses with uneven cash flows (although anybody can use the technique).

> **Example:** It is January 15th, and your fourth quarter estimated taxes are due. You must pay $4,000, but don't have the funds available. You know a $6,000 commission check will be issued to you on February 1st. You can if you choose withdraw the $4,00 you owe from your IRA and use it to pay your estimated taxes. When you receive your commission check in early February, simply deposit $4,000 in your IRA and the $2,000 balance wherever you normally would.

Note in this example that you didn't account for the interest on the money you borrowed. Not only is that not required, it's not allowed. The loan is, in effect, interest free. Of course, since you're borrowing from yourself, you are also losing the benefit of tax-deferred interest compounding while your funds are withdrawn. That's the first of several reasons why you should always redeposit borrowed IRA funds as quickly as possible.

A few critical warnings apply if you want to use this technique. First, be absolutely positive you will be able to replace the funds within 60 days. There is no flexibility here; 9:00 AM on the morning of the sixty-first day is too late. You will owe income tax, and the 10% penalty tax on the distribution if you're under 59-1/2. Also remember that the law says sixty days, not two months. If one of the two months in question has 31 days in it, you have one less calendar day in the next month to redeposit your funds.

> **Example:** You withdraw funds from an IRA on July 15th to finance a short-term loan. You have only until September 13th to re-deposit the funds you've withdrawn back into your old IRA (or to open a new one).

Second, you can only use this strategy once every twelve months regardless of how many IRAs you own. Plan ahead, because a second withdrawal will be taxable!

Lump-Sum Averaging

If you are younger, it is generally a good idea to roll over lump sum distributions you receive from an employer's retirement plan. However, there's a special rule (actually a set of rules) that can make it more advantageous for older "distributees" to pay tax on the earnings now.

The so-called "forward averaging" rules allow you to pay tax on a lump sum as if it were received over a number of years instead of all at once. You're allowed to "average" the payments over five years if you're 59-1/2 when you receive the lump sum. Even better, if you were born before 1936, you're allowed to average the payments over 10 years.

The method for computing the tax works something like this: divide the lump sum by 5 (or 10), apply the tax table to the result, and then multiply the result by 5 (or 10) again. Even though you actually pay the tax all in one year, these rules allow you to take advantage of the lower bracket 5 (or 10) times. The actual rules for computing forward averaging are a bit more complicated than this, and you likely will need the help of a tax consultant. To give you some idea of the benefits of averaging, however, consider the following simplified examples.

> **Example 1:** You received a taxable $150,000 lump-sum received in 1993. You are single. The tax due on this sum would be at least $42,522, applying the new tax rates now in effect. It could be more if you had other sources of income. However, the tax on $30,000, one-fifth of $150,000, would only be $5,527. Multiplied by five, the tax due if the $150,000 is forward-averaged over five years is only $27,635 ($5,527 x 5 = $27,635). This represents a savings of $14,887 ($42,522 - $27,635 = $14,887).

> **Example 2:** Use the same facts as above, except now assume that you qualify to average the lump sum over 10 years. The tax due on $15,000 (one-tenth of $150,000) is $2,457. Thus, the total tax due is $24,570 ($2,457 x 10). This represents a savings of $17,952 over the original tax of $42,522, and $3,065 over the five-year-averaged tax of $27,635.

There are, of course, restrictions applicable to forward averaging. The 10-year rule, in particular, can be tricky. It requires some special computations to be made regarding any pre-1974 capital gains included in your lump sum distribution, and is only available once in your lifetime. Both rules require that you be a plan participant for at least five years before receiving your lump-sum in order to qualify for averaging. Again, this is an area where expert assistance can quickly pay for itself.

There's another non-tax reason that it may make sense to take a lump-sum from an employer's plan when it's offered. If, when you retire, you are offered the choice of a lump sum or an annuity, you should probably take the lump sum, unless you have health problems or are poor at managing money. When your employer's plan pays you in the form of an annuity, it provides for a slightly lower return because it must assume the risk you will live longer than the actuarial tables say you will. You can increase that return by taking a lump sum and investing it, with the assistance of a trusted financial advisor.

A final note: lump-sum forward averaging is not available for retirement savings contained in an IRA, and is available on a somewhat limited basis for funds in a Keogh.

Minimum Distributions

As a general rule, the longer you allow your retirement assets to enjoy the benefits of tax-deferred compounding, the better. (The lump-sum averaging rules, discussed above, are one possible exception to this rule.) However, eventually the tax law requires you to begin making withdrawals from your retirement accounts or face yet another penalty for failing to do so. Worse yet, the penalty is equal to a whopping 50% of the amount you were supposed to withdraw. It is therefore critically important to understand the minimum distribution rules.

By April 1st of the year after you reach age 70-1/2, you must begin withdrawing from your retirement savings in order to avoid penalties. The rules require you to withdraw the money over your life expectancy, which you can find by consulting IRS tables. Since life expectancies vary by gender, there are different tables for men and women. For instance, at age 70, according to recent IRS tables, a man has a life expectancy of 12.1 years, while a woman has an expectancy of 15 years. The net effect of this rule is to require you to annuitize your account balances.

> **Example:** You are a female born on 1 July, 1923. You have $75,000 in an IRA account. You turn 70-1/2 on 1 December, 1993, and by 1 April, 1994 must begin to make withdrawals from your IRA. Since your life expectancy is 15 years, your first withdrawal must be at least $5,000 ($75,000/15 = $5,000). This amount must be included in your income for the year.

There are a few things you can do to soften the sting of the minimum distribution rules, assuming you would prefer not to have to withdraw and pay tax on your retirement funds. First, you can re-compute your minimum distribution each year. Since average life expectancies increase slightly each year, this may lower slightly your minimum distribution for the year.

Next, if you designate a beneficiary for your account(s), you can use either a joint life expectancy or your beneficiary's life expectancy alone. To qualify for the latter option, your life expectancy and your beneficiary's must be within 10 years of each other. Using a younger beneficiary results in greater life expectancy rates and thus smaller required distributions. Again, this is a good area in which to seek the assistance of a tax advisor.

RETIREMENT PLAN TRAPS

You've worked hard all your life, put the maximum amount of savings possible into contributory retirement plans (i.e., 401(k)s, IRAs), and generally done everything your advisors have told you to do and the tax laws encourage you to do in planning for your golden years. Then, one day, perhaps when you retire, you decide to take a large distribution from your retirement plans. When informed about your distribution, your advisor reports that you will have to pay a 15% penalty tax because you've accumulated *too much* by way of retirement savings!

Too much??? "I thought Americans were encouraged to increase their savings", you think to yourself, incredulously. Believe it or not, there are two separate penalties you have to worry about if you accumulate too much in tax-deferred retirement accounts.

The first penalty tax applies if you withdraw too much from your account at once. The good news is that the amounts involved are very high -- the tax kicks in above $150,000 in regular withdrawals during any year, and above $750,000 in lump-sum distributions (The difference between periodic withdrawals and lump-sum distributions was discussed in the last section). Eventually, these figures will be indexed for inflation.

> **Example 1:** You retire at age 65 with a $250,000 balance in your 401(k) plan. You decide to withdraw $175,000 from the plan in order to purchase a new residence in a retirement community. In addition to paying income tax on the amount you withdraw, you will owe a $3,750 penalty tax on the $25,000 in excess of the $150,000 annual limit on withdrawals ($25,000 x 15% = $3,750).
>
> **Example 2:** You retire at age 65 with an $800,000 balance in your defined benefit retirement plan. Rather than receiving an annuity from your employer or rolling the funds over into an IRA, you elect a lump-sum distribution of the entire accrued benefit. In addition to the income tax

on the $800,000, you will owe a $7,500 penalty tax on the $50,000 by which you've exceeded the $750,000 "limit" on lump-sum distributions ($50,000 x 15% = $7,500).

Note that, in the second example, it may still be beneficial to take the lump-sum distribution and pay the penalty. This is because the benefits of forward-averaging available for lump-sum distributions may outweigh the amount of the penalty tax you will be required to pay. This will vary somewhat depending on your overall financial and tax picture. So, if either of these taxes applies to you, spend some time with a financial advisor working the math before deciding what to do with your pension.

The second penalty tax applies to excess retirement plan accumulations in your estate when you die. The threshold for imposing the penalty on these accumulations varies with your life expectancy, and the tax is only levied on the excess of what an annuity would pay over that expectancy.

Example: You are a 70 year old male. According to IRS, a hypothetical annuity currently is paying 10%. IRS tables indicate your actuarial life expectancy is a little less six and one-half years. If you were to die today, your applicable threshold would be $961,395. Any money above that amount in your retirement plans would be hit with the 15% penalty tax.

This example gives you a good idea of the "price range" involved. As a rough rule of thumb, multiply your life expectancy by $150,000; that is your applicable threshold. Remember, however, that it's the excess in your accounts when you die that gets taxed. Since your life expectancy goes down as you get older, so will your threshold. The tax, of course, is paid by your estate, but it is in addition to any other estate taxes you will owe.

Keep in mind that these rules are applied at the aggregate level. That is, they apply to all of your retirement plans combined -- IRAs, Keoghs, 401(k)s and company pension plans all must be considered when determining if you've accumulated too much.

There are a couple of things you can do to avoid these taxes if you think you may be affected by them. First, keep track of your account balances and don't let them rise above the $750,000 limit. If you sense you're getting close, stop making discretionary contributions where possible.

> **Example:** You are 55 years old, and employed by a large company which offers both a pension plan and a 401(k) plan; you contribute the maximum amount allowed by law to the latter. You also own a few IRA accounts from the days when contributions to them were fully tax deductible. The combined balances in all of your accounts are $715,000. You should consider ending or reducing the elective contributions to your 401(k) plan in order to stay below the $750,000 limit.

There's a second (and perhaps better) technique available if you are affected by the excess accumulations tax. If you are approaching the $750,000 limit, begin making withdrawals as soon as you hit age 59-1/2. This allows you to avoid the 10% penalty on premature distributions (discussed in the last section), and also helps you avoid the 15% penalty tax on excess accumulations.

> **Example:** You are 60 years old, with $60,000 in your IRA accounts and an accrued benefit of $675,000 in your employer's retirement plan. You conservatively estimate that your employer will accrue $15,000 per year more to your benefit in each of the next five years before you reach age 65. If you withdraw $12,000 from your IRA in each of the next five years, your total retirement accumulations will fall just short of the $750,000 threshold. This will enable you to elect a lump sum on your pension and forward average the income without incurring the 15% penalty tax, should you choose to do so. Remember, though, you will have to pay income tax (but not the 10% penalty tax on premature withdrawals) on the $12,000.

In this example, you were encouraged to take five smaller distributions from your IRA in each of the next five years instead of just liquidating the account in the fifth year. By spreading the withdrawals out over a period of time, you minimize the chances that the extra income will put you in a higher tax bracket. Again, figuring out exactly how much to withdraw will depend on your overall circumstances, and can be tricky, so you're well advised to get professional help in crunching your particular numbers. Of course, if you expect to live long enough to spend your retirement accounts down under the threshold that applies to you, you may not need to plan around this penalty.